WISDOM OF THE KADAM MASTERS

WISDOM OF THE
KADAM MASTERS

Translated, edited, and introduced by

Thupten Jinpa

WISDOM PUBLICATIONS • BOSTON

Wisdom Publications
199 Elm Street
Somerville, MA 02144 USA
www.wisdompubs.org

Library of Congress Cataloging-in-Publication Data

Wisdom of the Kadam masters / translated, edited, and introduced by Thupten Jinpa.
    pages cm. — (Tibetan classics)
  Includes bibliographical references and index.
  ISBN 1-61429-054-7 (pbk. : alk. paper)
  1. Bka'-gdams-pa (Sect)—Doctrines. I. Thupten Jinpa, translator, editor of compilation, writer of added commentary.
  BQ7670.4W57 2013
  294.3'4432—dc23

                            2012044496

ISBN 978-1-61429-054-4
eBook ISBN 978-1-61429-065-0

17 16 15 14 13
5 4 3 2 1

Cover design by Phil Pascuzzo. Interior design by Gopa & Ted2, Inc. Set in Dia-
critical Garamond Pro 10.7/12.7. Cover image is "Two Kadam Masters with Their
Lineages, 12th Century." (From an anonymous collection.)

Wisdom Publications' books are printed on acid-free paper and meet the guidelines
for permanence and durability of the Production Guidelines for Book Longevity of
the Council on Library Resources.

Printed in the United States of America.

This book was produced with environmental mindfulness. We have elected to print this title on 30% PCW
recycled paper. As a result, we have saved the following
resources: 12 trees, 5 million BTUs of energy, 870 lbs. of greenhouse gases, 5,264
gallons of water, and 353 lbs. of solid waste. For more information, please visit our
website, www.wisdompubs.org. This paper is also FSC® certified. For more information, please visit www.fscus.org.

Publisher's Acknowledgment

THE PUBLISHER gratefully acknowledges the generous help of the Hershey Family Foundation in sponsoring the publication of this book.

Contents

Preface

WISDOM OF THE KADAM MASTERS is the second volume in the new series *Tibetan Classics*, which aims to make available accessible paperback editions of key Tibetan Buddhist works in English translation. The main selection in this volume is the much-loved twelfth-century work known as *Sayings of the Kadam Masters*. That these celebrated sayings continue to resonate powerfully for those on the spiritual path nearly a millennium after their utterance shows that they capture something profound about our yearning. The next three selections in this special anthology, chapters from the Father Teachings of the *Book of Kadam*, present lively exchanges between the Indian master Atiśa and his Tibetan heir, Dromtönpa. The final selection is a chapter from the Son Teachings of the *Book of Kadam*, an entertaining tale of one of Master Drom's previous lives.

These selections, so revered in the Tibetan tradition, have been drawn from the larger hardcover volume entitled *The Book of Kadam: The Core Texts*, which I had the privilege to translate into English for *The Library of Tibetan Classics*. In this volume, however, I have expanded the contextualizing materials for the general reader. These include a general introduction, explanations specific to each of the three sections, biographical notes on the authors whose sayings are featured in the volume, as well as an explanatory glossary. Together, these materials provide historical and cultural context as well as an overview of the central themes of the individual texts, allowing the reader to engage with the words in a more meaningful way.

I would like to express my deep gratitude, first and foremost, to my two spiritual teachers, His Holiness the Dalai Lama and the late Kyabjé Zemé Rinpoché, both of whom helped bring the teachings of the Kadam masters to life for me. My heartfelt thanks go to Barry Hershey, Connie Hershey, and the Hershey Family Foundation, whose support made it possible for me to translate the larger volume from which the texts selected here were drawn. I must also thank Pierre and Pamela Omidyar, who through a special grant enabled me to develop this particular volume for general readers.

Let me also take this opportunity to express my deep appreciation to Nita Ing and the Ing Family Foundation and to Eric Colombel and the Tsadra Foundation for their ongoing support of translating multiple volumes from *The Library of Tibetan Classics*. I also thank David Kittelstrom, our longtime editor at Wisdom Publications on the classics series, for his incisive editing of my English; Tim McNeill and his team at Wisdom for their dedication to excellence; and my wife Sophie Boyer Langri for her unwavering support of my work.

Thupten Jinpa
Montreal, 2012

Introduction

"Even if we try to do something, what needs doing
beyond simply observing our own minds?
—GÖNPAWA[1]

THE PHRASE "the Kadam masters" evokes, for many Tibetans like myself who grew up within a monastic environment, a sense of a spiritual golden age in Tibet—an idyllic image of a spiritual community consisting of wise monks dedicated to a life of deep spiritual quest and mental cultivation with a sense of abandon and total freedom. These Tibetan masters are famed particularly for their pithy spiritual sayings, short poignant utterances that capture essential teachings in digestible bites. In these sayings one unmistakably detects a note of courage and decisiveness, an absence of confusion about the priorities of a well-lived life, as well as a clear understanding of what a truly happy life consists of, all grounded in an uncompromising adherence to the altruistic ideal of universal compassion—a deeply felt, genuine concern for the welfare of all beings. The spirit of these pithy sayings are illustrated by the following well-known saying:

Inside the house of a person with a sense of abandon
sleeps someone who is totally at ease;
those ridden with hopes and fears fail to notice this.

Inside the house of a person who is content
sleeps someone who is truly rich;
those ridden with greed fail to notice this.[2]

These lines succinctly convey with powerful imagery two universal spiritual principles—(1) that a mind no longer imprisoned in the perpetual cycle of expectations, hopes, and fears is a mind that is truly at ease, and (2) that those who are contented in mind are truly rich, for no matter how much we might have materially, we are not rich in the truest sense of the word if we still crave for more. In contrast, a mind caught in obsessive self-focused thoughts of hopes and fears is robbed of any space for happiness to take root. Similarly, a perpetually discontented state of mind chained to craving for more is deprived of any chance to truly appreciate what one has and instead focuses negatively on what one does not.

Today modern science is increasingly coming to recognize the crucial role our minds play in determining the quality of our lives, especially when it comes to questions of happiness and suffering. To a large extent, the way we experience the world is significantly shaped by the way we see ourselves and the world around us, and by the attitudes and values with which we relate to both. This, in turn, influences how we act and react. His Holiness the Dalai Lama often reminds his audiences of the need to appreciate how the most important factor for personal happiness lies within. Yes, material facilities are important; yes, companionship, good health, and good reputation are also important factors of happiness. None of these guarantee our happiness. In contrast, if we have a genuine inner peace, then even in the midst of material hardships we can maintain a sense of well-being. Most of what the Kadam masters have to say, in one way or another, relates to this important nexus of thought, emotion, and action.

When the Kadam master Gönpawa was on his deathbed, we

are told, he gave the following four brief counsels to his grieving disciple Phuchungwa:

> Teach others what you practice;
> practice what you preach;
> even at a place where you might be staying for a single day, do not act as an outside guest but constantly remember your teachers and their instructions;
> and always cultivate limitless loving-kindness toward other sentient beings.[3]

Once again, in a few simple lines we see important universal spiritual principles echoed with great efficiency. "Teach others what *you* practice" underlines the important ethos that we should only teach others things that we ourselves have gained some degree of mastery in. In spiritual matters, it shouldn't be the case of the blind leading the blind. "Practice what you preach" encapsulates the important principle that, in matters of spiritual practice, the teacher is as much a student as his disciples. This line echoes one of the four factors of sustaining other's minds—namely, "acting in accord with your own advice." The advice that we should not act as an outside guest even at a place where we might happen to stay only for a day makes the point that when it comes to mindful awareness, there is no place or occasion for exceptions. A true spiritual practitioner will not use being away from his or her normal meditative environment as an excuse for laxity. Finally, Master Gönpawa reminds us that at the end of the day what matters most is caring for the needs and welfare of other sentient beings—the practice of loving-kindness.

One well-known Kadam saying is Master Ben Güngyal's encapsulation of what he saw to be the heart of a spiritual practitioner's task. He states, "I have no task other than to stand guard at the gate of the afflictions' fortress, holding the spear of the antidotes. If the afflictions are vigilant, I remain vigilant. If they are relaxed, I remain relaxed."[4] In essence, what Ben Güngyal is saying is this: the heart of the spiritual aspirant's practice is to cultivate greater self-awareness, especially with respect to thoughts and emotions, and to learn to deal with internal dissonances on that basis. I particularly like the imagery of standing guard at the gateway of the mind. For through our mind we not only interact with the world, but to a large extent, we create it. Contemporary research in the psychological sciences is increasingly confirming the basic insight of contemplatives: our perceptions and attitudes with regard to ourselves and the world shape our experiences of them. So if we can learn to acquire a skill that enables us to monitor what comes in and what goes out through the gateway of the mind, we then have a real chance to bring our deeper aspirations and values to bear upon our relationship with ourselves, with others, and with the world around us. Greater control over the mind opens up a whole new way of being in the world and allows a genuine freedom to live our lives in accord with our deeper aspirations, unhindered by the instincts and impulses that can pull us in the contrary directions. For a spiritual aspirant, this is a freedom with real meaning.

I first came across some of these Kadam sayings when, as a twelve-year-old young monk in Dharamsala, India, I had the opportunity to attend a month-long teaching given by His Holiness the Dalai Lama on Tsongkhapa's classic *Stages on the Path to Enlightenment*. It was a time when everyone, including the Dalai Lama himself, seemed to have plenty of time. Dharamsala, where His Holiness had established his residence in the early 1960s soon after his arrival in India as a refugee, was then a beautiful and quiet place. If my calculation is correct, this teaching took place in the spring of 1971. Needless to say, most of what His Holiness taught was way above the comprehension of a twelve-year-old boy, no matter how certain he might have been of his own intelligence. What struck me powerfully at this series of teaching was the depth of His Holiness's reverence—

one might even say deep affection—for the life and sayings of the Tibetan Kadam masters. The text the Dalai Lama was teaching on that occasion is well known for being filled with pithy spiritual sayings, especially those of the early Kadam masters. One day the Dalai Lama spoke about what the Kadam masters called the "four entrustments":

Entrust your mind to Dharma practice;
entrust your Dharma practice to a life of poverty;
entrust your life of poverty to death;
and entrust your death to an empty cave.[5]

To our modern sensibilities these are admittedly quite radical sentiments. Yet one cannot deny the note of clarity and decisiveness in these lines, especially in evocation of the powerful ideal of true nonattachment. We are being admonished not only to turn our mind to spirituality but to actually entrust the entire focus of our mind to spirituality if we are serious about seeking the highest spiritual goal. And when we do so, we are instructed to proceed with such dedication that the pursuit of material gain never enters our calculations. The third line, "entrust your life of poverty to death," advises us that the pursuit of a spiritual path through a life of poverty should not be only a temporary means but a way of life to be embraced until our final end. When that end comes, we should not be concerned about what might happen to our body. Instead, we should have the attitude that "like the carcass of a dead animal, if our body ends up lying in a barren cave, so be it."

As the Dalai Lama spoke of these sentiments, astonishingly (at least to the eyes of a twelve-year-old boy) His Holiness wept in front of the entire congregation of several hundred monks. He spoke of how the sentiments expressed in the principle of the four entrustments lay before us as spiritual aspirants. That sentiment is one of the highest ideals—a life truly dedicated to meditative cultivation, with total freedom and transcendence. The Dalai Lama then expressed how lines such as these exerted a powerful pull on his heart and that the challenge for him was how to balance a life dedicated to meditative cultivation with service to others. Fourteen years later, in the autumn of 1985, I had the unexpected honor of being asked to translate at a teaching His Holiness conducted in the very same hall. Thus began my totally unimagined opportunity to serve the Dalai Lama and, through him, to serve the world—an honor that has continued for more than a quarter of a century now.

Since that spring of 1971, I have had numerous opportunities as a young monk to receive formal instructions on *lamrim* (stages of the path) and *lojong* (mind training)—the two trademark spiritual teachings of the Kadampas—from such senior Tibetan masters as the two tutors of His Holiness the Dalai Lama as well as from my own personal teacher, Kyabjé Zemé Rinpoché. The junior tutor to His Holiness, Kyabjé Trijang Rinpoché, was particularly adept at weaving his instructions with stories and bringing the pithy sayings of the Kadam masters to life, a feat that made listening to his teachings a real feast for the mind and heart. Like poignant lines from favorite poems that come to be part of one's memory, some of these sayings became over time part of my mental landscape and continue to resonate powerfully for me on a personal level.

Who Are the Kadam Masters?

"Kadampa" refers to a wide range of Tibetan Buddhists who share a particular reverence for the person and teachings of the Indian master Atiśa and his Tibetan spiritual heir Dromtönpa.[6] Atiśa was an Indian Bengali teacher who came to Tibet in the summer of 1042 and lived in the Land of Snows for nearly thirteen years, never to return home to India. His arrival in Tibet was part of what Tibetan historians call the "second diffusion of Buddhism"—the beginnings of a large-scale revival of Buddhism in Tibet in the aftermath of its decline during the reign of Tibet's last emperor, Langdarma, and the collapse of the central Tibetan kingdom in the tenth century. By the middle of the eleventh century, Tibet had splintered into several kingdoms, with descendants of the imperial family ruling over some of these kingdoms. The kingdom of Ngari in the west was one such domain, and its rulers were instrumental in bringing Atiśa to Tibet.

For Tibetans Atiśa's arrival on their soil was an occasion for celebration, as it marked the culmination of years of sacrifice of both personal and material resources for the purpose of bringing an Indian master of his stature to Tibet. The Indian master was received on the Nepalese side of the border by a welcoming party of around three hundred horsemen from Tibet, recalling the Tibetan reception of the grand abbot Śāntarakṣita several centuries earlier.[7] Before he touched Tibetan soil, Atiśa must already have become familiar with the broad historical outline of Tibet's relation to Buddhism—the role of the famous Indian Buddhist philosopher Śāntarakṣita, especially his introduction of the monastic order; the founding of the first monastery, Samyé, in central Tibet; and the efforts of early Tibetan translators to transmit classical Indian Buddhist texts to Tibet. Atiśa spent three years in the western Tibetan kingdom of Ngari. It appears that as part of the conditions for letting Atiśa go to Tibet, the Tibetan translator Naktso Lotsāwa had to give his word to the abbot of Vikramaśila Monastery that he would bring Atiśa back after three years. So, after the three years were over, despite entreaties from Tibetan disciples (especially from Dromtönpa) who were keen to bring Atiśa to central Tibet, Naktso insisted that they honor the solemn pledge he had given to the abbot and bring Atiśa back to India. Thus Atiśa and his entourage began the journey back home. Fortunately for Tibet, however, the way back through Nepal turned out to be unsafe due to some regional war. This provided a legitimate excuse for Naktso—Atiśa telling him, "There is no sin in failing a pledge that cannot be honored"—who then agreed with others that the master should go to central Tibet, the historically important region near Lhasa.

Once Master Atiśa headed for central Tibet, with the exception of a brief initial sojourn to visit his student Khutön, a wealthy and powerful lama, Dromtönpa took charge of the master's itinerary. Thus began Atiśa's second mission in Tibet. The master taught extensively, guided an entire generation of disciples committed to meditative cultivation, collaborated in projects of translating more classical Indian Buddhist texts into Tibetan, and composed independent works on Buddhist thought and practice. On a personal level, Atiśa is said to have enjoyed his time in Tibet. He was so taken by the purity and the sweet taste of water on the Tibetan plateau that, it is widely believed, it was he who began the Tibetan custom of making daily offerings of water in bowls in front of altars. We also read in the master's biographies that he extolled the virtues of the Tibetan custom of drinking tea. When I first read this I was especially intrigued, for drinking tea is so widespread today on the Indian plains where I grew up. Later I found out that it was only during the British colonial period that tea became part of Indian culture, which allowed me to appreciate Atiśa's comments about tea drinking.

Master Atiśa's contribution to Buddhism in Tibet was so deeply appreciated by his Tibetan followers that he came to be referred to by the epithet "the lord" (*jowo*) or "the sole lord" (*lhachik*). Over time the sacrifices and efforts made by the rulers of Ngari to bring Atiśa to Tibet also came to be mythologized, becoming part of an important narrative of the history of Buddhadharma in the Land of Snows. Just as the story of the Chinese monk Xuan Tsang's travel to India in search of Buddhist scriptures was popularized in the legend entitled *Journey to the*

West, the story of how the kings of Ngari made extensive sacrifices to bring Atiśa to Tibet were popularized in narratives and plays that are still performed to this day. Atiśa passed away in 1054 at his favorite retreat of Nyethang, nearly thirteen years after he first set foot on Tibetan soil.

Following Atiśa's death his Tibetan followers found a locus for their identification as members of a distinct community in Radreng Monastery, founded by Atiśa's spiritual heir Dromtönpa in 1056. These members came to describe themselves as the Kadampas, a designation composed of two words covering a wide semantic range—*ka* refers to sacred words or speech, and *dam* refers either to advice and instruction or to the verbs "to bind" and "to choose."

A fifteenth-century history of the Kadam order offers four different explanations of the name.[8] First, *Kadam* may be defined as "those for whom the essence of the entire Buddhist scripture is integrated within the path of the three scopes—the spiritual aspirations of initial, intermediate, and advance capacities—and for whom all the scriptures of the Buddha appear as personal instructions." A second interpretation of the meaning of *Kadam* suggests that the tradition is so called "because the Kadam founding father, Dromtönpa, chose, in accordance with the sacred instruction of Master Atiśa, the *sevenfold divinity and teaching* as his principal practice." "Sevenfold" refers to the threefold teaching (the baskets of monastic discipline, discourses, and knowledge) and the four divinities (Buddha, Avaloliteśvara, Tārā, and Acala). A third interpretation is that when Master Atiśa was residing at Nyethang his disciples accorded great authority to his sacred words, so they came to be known as "Kadampas"—those who hold the sacred words as binding. The final interpretation is that the Kadampas are guided by the three baskets of scripture in their overall Dharma practice and approach Vajrayana teachings and practices circumspectly.

By the middle of the twelfth century, about a century after Master Atiśa's death, the spiritual descendants of the master and his heir Dromtönpa—the Kadampas—had spread far and wide. Many of the early teachers established monasteries and retreats in different parts of central and western Tibet. In summing up the influence of the Kadam tradition on Tibetan Buddhism as a whole, the authoritative *Blue Annals* states:

> In general, during Master Atiśa's thirteen years in Tibet, a vast number received essential instructions from him and attained higher Dharma qualities. Their precise number cannot be calculated. In Tsang was the trio Gar, Gö, and Yöl, while in central Tibet was the trio Khu, Ngok, and Drom. These are masters of great fame. Here, however, I have given a broad account of the spiritual mentors whose lineage stems from Drom and whose names I have seen myself. Otherwise, according to their biographies, most of spiritual mentors who appeared in Tibet subsequently as well as the yogis who engaged in the life of an adept appeared to have studied at the feet of a Kadam spiritual mentor. Therefore Drom was someone whose enlightened activities were extensive and long lasting.[9]

Atiśa's Kadam Legacy

Master Atiśa is perhaps revered most in Tibetan Buddhism for his genius in distilling the essence of the teachings of the Buddha into the framework of a single spiritual aspirant's path. His *Lamp for the Path to Enlightenment*, which was composed, as its colophon states, at the explicit request of the Ngari ruler Jangchup Ö, organizes the entire corpus of the Buddhist teachings into what he calls practices relevant to "persons of three scopes" or "persons of three capacities"—initial, intermediate, and great. This revolutionary approach to understanding the heterogeneous literature of the Indian Buddhist sources enabled the Tibetans to appropriately contextualize and integrate the knowledge of these sources meaningfully within an individual's meditative practice. Over time an entire genre of literature, collectively known as *stages of the path* or *lamrim*, evolved in Tibet on the basis of this seminal work by Atiśa. A key feature of the lamrim texts is their graduated approach to the path to enlightenment.

The second genre of literature that evolved in Tibet from Atiśa's teachings is the cycle of *mind-training* or *lojong* texts, the most well known of which are Atiśa's own *Bodhisattva's Jewel Garland*, Langri Thangpa's (1054–1123) *Eight Verses on Mind Training*, and the *Seven-Point Mind Training*, the latter being traditionally attributed to Chekawa (1101–75). The focal point of mind-training teachings is the cultivation of the *awakening mind* (*bodhicitta*), especially in the tradition of Śāntideva's (eighth century) "equalizing and exchanging self and others." This cultivation often employs the practice of *tonglen*, or "giving and receiving." The heart of tonglen involves imaginatively "receiving" or taking upon oneself the suffering, unhappiness, and basic negative emotional and thought patterns of others, and "giving" or offering to others one's own happiness, good fortune, and positive mental states. Unlike the stages of the path teachings, mind training emphasizes the use of pithy sayings and a direct approach when dealing with obstacles to the development of the awakening mind, the altruistic aspiration to attain full enlightenment for the benefit of all beings.

Perhaps the most intriguing set of teachings that traces its origin to Master Atiśa is the collection enshrined in two large volumes known together as the *Book of Kadam*, selections of which are translated in the present volume. This cycle of texts relates

Atiśa's special relationship with Dromtönpa and highlights many of the more mystical aspects of Atiśa's legacy in Tibet, especially his veneration of Avalokiteśvara, the buddha of compassion, and his propitiation of goddess Tārā. Known as Atiśa and Dromtönpa's "secret teachings," this set of texts is centered on the choice of four meditation deities—(1) the Buddha as the teacher, (2) Avalokiteśvara as the deity of compassion, (3) Tārā as the goddess of enlightened action, and (4) Acala as the protector guardian—and the three scriptural baskets of discipline, knowledge, and meditation. This particular set of teachings is significant because of the ways in which it creates shifts in focus from the source teachings. For example, with respect to the teacher, the focus of importance shifts from Master Atiśa to Dromtönpa; with respect to land, it shifts from India as the land of Dharma to Tibet as a place of special significance connected with Avalokiteśvara; and with regard to spiritual instructions, although the Kadam period heralded the systematic scholastic study of the great Indian Buddhist classics, the focus shifts from classical Indian scriptures and treatises to the master's direct oral teachings, especially as revealed in mystic visionary states. There is a shift even in the style of language employed from classical composition to a more informal style, with greater use of vernacular Tibetan.

One intriguing issue in the history of the Kadam order is its disappearance. Although more research is needed to confirm this, it seems that by the end of sixteenth century, Kadam effectively ceased to be a distinct school. This may partly be due to the tremendous success of the custodians of Atiśa and Dromtönpa's teachings, on account of which all the key elements of the Kadam teachings were incorporated into the teachings of other Tibetan schools. It may also be partly the result of the rapid growth of Tsongkhapa's (1357–1419) Geluk school. Initially referred to as the Gandenpas after Ganden Monastery was founded by Tsongkhapa in 1409, Gelukpas were referred to also as the "new Kadampas."

Conclusion

The teachings of the Kadam masters have spiritually nourished the Tibetan people for nearly a millennium and have helped to shape our deeper aspirations. These teachings have helped to moisten the heart so that the seeds of compassion can sprout into beautiful shoots of altruistic awakening minds. They have helped to educate minds so that they see the world in a wiser, more enlightened manner. And finally, they have helped guide the spirit so that it continues to be moved by aspirations for the highest possible human perfection—namely the attainment of buddhahood for the benefit of all beings. It is wonderfully gratifying that through volumes such as this we are able to share with members of the larger world community this precious heritage of the Tibetan people, so that spiritual aspirants of all backgrounds may be able to drink from the stream of this spiritual nectar. Admittedly, many of the wise counsels of the Tibetan Kadam masters are framed within a language and culture specific to the Tibetan Buddhist world. Nonetheless, they also undeniably embody insights and knowledge that are universal and appeal to our fundamental nature as human beings aspiring for peace and happiness.

Of the various elements of the Kadam heritage, two stand out for me personally as continual sources of deep inspiration and spiritual nourishment. One is the teachings on *lojong* or mind training, and the other is the collection known as the "sayings of the Kadam masters." What makes these two sets of teachings particularly attractive are their characteristic down-to-earthness, their succinctness, and their unwavering advocacy for cultivating other-regarding altruistic instincts.

I have had the honor of presenting the first of these two genres of Kadam teachings to a more general readership in a previous compilation entitled *Essential Mind Training*. The present volume, *Wisdom of the Kadam Masters*, is aimed at sharing the second genre with a broader audience. The volume is divided into two parts. Part I presents the celebrated twelfth-century *Sayings of the Kadam Masters*, often referred to simply as the "Scattered Sayings." It was compiled by Master Chegom to ensure that these sayings, originally dispersed among many people, were not lost and forgotten. Part II presents four chapters selected from the *Book of Kadam*: the first three from the Father Teachings (a series of dialogues between Master Atiśa and Dromtönpa in twenty-three chapters) and the final a sample chapter from the Son Teachings (a collection of stories of Dromtönpa's previous lives as narrated by Master Atiśa). For more specific aspects of these two parts, see my introduction to part II. Translations of these classical Tibetan texts are all drawn from the much larger volume entitled *The Book of Kadam: The Core Texts*, which I had the honor to translate and publish as part of *The Library of Tibetan Classics*.

Although these Tibetan teachings emerged nearly a thousand years ago within a specific historical cultural context, like many of the world's great spiritual teachings, the teachings of the Kadam masters embody insights and wisdom that resonate beyond the boundaries of time, culture, and language. This volume offers to modern-day Buddhists some of the most beloved teachings of the Tibetan tradition in an accessible format. For practitioners of other religious traditions, the texts collected in this special anthology will provide a glimpse into the rich world of Tibetan Buddhist teaching and practice and may offer insights and approaches that could be incorporated into the practices of one's own cherished faith. To those readers who have no particular religious inclination, these teachings could be approached as a portion of the accumulated wisdom of humanity, representative of the long history of the human quest to better understand our existence and its meaning.

PART I

Sayings of the Kadam Masters

WISE WORDS

Sayings of the Kadam Masters is a unique collection of pithy statements uttered by Tibetan teachers containing spiritual advice and reflections on life, mental cultivation, and the Buddhist quest for true enlightenment. These sayings, which are attributed to some of the greatest spiritual masters of Tibet, cover a wide range of themes of deep interest to spiritual aspirants, such as:

- The balance between individual cultivation and compassionate action in the world
- The balance and dynamic relationship among study, critical reflection, and meditation
- The relationship between wisdom and compassion
- The cultivation of greater self-awareness, especially in relation to our thoughts and emotions
- The principles of nonattachment and nongrasping
- The contemplation of death and impermanence
- The practice of self-discipline
- The way to bring the teaching of no-self into actual lived experience
- The way to integrate our outlook with contemplative practice and action in the world—a triad referred to as "view, meditation, and action"
- Contemplative practices aimed at developing the four immeasurable thoughts of loving-kindness, compassion, joy, and equanimity

Like the "Sayings of the Desert Fathers" of the early Christian church, these sayings of the Kadam masters have stood the test of time and have continued to provide a deep source of inspiration to seekers of truth. The essence of these teachings, beyond their specific cultural and temporal provenance, continues to resonate poignantly even in today's fast-paced technological age. If anything, these teachings are even more relevant today, because they provide contemporary people facing complex challenges and endless distractions a glimpse into the space of tranquility, contentment, and deep connectedness that the human mind is capable of. Indeed such inner cultivation may be vital for the survival of the human race.

Ever since their emergence in the Land of Snows during the first century of the second millennium, the teachings of the Kadam masters have not only nurtured the spiritual aspirations of so many seekers of truth, they have shaped and defined the spiritual aspirations and sensibilities of an entire civilization. From the eleventh century onward, every Tibetan work of spiritual instruction, especially those relating to the cultivation of universal compassion and the bodhisattva's altruistic ideal, or of philosophical enquiry into the nature of ultimate wisdom has been thoroughly informed by the teachings of the Kadam masters. Whether they are the writings of Gampopa (a founding father of the Kagyü lineage), Sakya luminaries such as Sakya Paṇḍita, Ngülchu Thokmé Sangpo (author of the famed *Thirty-Seven Verses on the Bodhisattva Practice*), the great Nyingma teacher Longchenpa, or Tsongkhapa (founder of the Geluk school), all subsequent great Tibetan teachers owe a deep debt to the wisdom and teachings of the Kadam masters.

Chegom Sherap Dorjé, also known as the adept Chegom, originally put together our present text in the twelfth century. In his editor's colophon to the collection, Master Chegom writes, "Here, the monk Chegom has briefly collected and compiled the sayings of the Kadam masters, which represent the heart advice of the sublime teachers of Master Atiśa's lineage that had previously been scattered." When I was a student monk at Ganden Monastery in South India, my personal teacher Kyabjé Dzemé Rinpoché gave me a traditional xylograph copy of the *Scattered Sayings*. It was a woodblock edition printed at the famous Shöl Printing Press in Lhasa. Since then this short text has been one of my most cherished works, a text that I always keep coming back to. I will often select a random passage from the text and read it in the morning as a thought for the day.

Chegom was an important Kadam master in his own right. He was a principal disciple of Jangchup Nangwa, who was in turn a student of Master Potowa. In the history of Tibetan spiritual literature, however, Chegom is honored more for his authorship of a trio of texts collectively referred to as "the three heaps": (1) the *Jewel Heap of Teachings through Similes*, a lucid commentary on a root text composed by Master Potowa, (2) the *Jewel Heap of Pith Instructions*, a unique text weaving the Kadam instructions with the Mahāmudrā teachings, and (3) the *Jewel Heap of Practices*, a work no longer extant. Among his writings there is also a beautiful and moving work in verse entitled *Lamp for the Fortunate Ones*, a collection of advice for hermits living a way of life dedicated to single-pointed meditative practice.

The *Scattered Sayings* text is structured around three clusters, the first two dedicated to the sayings of the founding fathers of the Kadam tradition—Atiśa and Drom—followed by selected sayings from other Tibetan masters of the Kadam lineage—the immediate disciples of the founding fathers, such as Master Gönpawa and the three Kadam brothers (Potowa, Chengawa, and Phuchungwa), and second-generation Kadam teachers like Neusurpa and others.

It appears that other additions were made to the collection soon after its original compilation. The first was a cluster of sayings particular to Master Kharakpa organized in numerical sets as compiled by his disciple Geshé Lhopa. Later a selection of sayings by Master Chegom, the editor of our original collection, appears to have been added to the text. It is difficult to determine based on the material available when this final piece was added.

SAYINGS OF THE KADAM MASTERS

Compiled by Chegom Sherap Dorjé

Herein lie the scattered sayings of the sublime masters
of Kadam. Respectfully I pay homage
to the sublime teachers.

1. The Sayings of Master Atiśa

ONCE WHEN the great master Atiśa, the sole lord, visited central Tibet, his three disciples Khutön, Ngok, and Dromtönpa[10] asked the following question: "Atiśa, in order for a practitioner to attain liberation and the state of omniscience, which is the more important of the two—the sutras and their commentarial treatises or the teachers' essential instructions?"

Atiśa replied, "Essential instructions are more important than the treatises."

When asked, "Why?" he replied, "Even if one can recite the three baskets of scripture by heart and is versed in the definitions of all phenomena, at the time of actual meditative practice, if one lacks the application of the [essential instruction of the] teaching, the teaching and the person will remain separate from each other."

They then reported, "If one were to thoroughly condense the way to apply the essential instructions of the teachers, it appears to be abiding in the three vows and striving in the virtues through one's three doors. Is this not so?"

Atiśa responded: "Even if you abide in accord with the three vows and remain pure, as long as your mind is not disenchanted with the three realms of cyclic existence, you will create the conditions for turning the wheel again. Also, even if you strive through your three doors in the virtues both day and night, if you lack the knowledge of how to dedicate them toward full awakening, they will be eroded through some distorted conceptualization. Even if you are a learned scholar, a disciplined practitioner, a teacher, or a meditator, if you fail to turn your thoughts away from the eight mundane concerns, whatever you do will be directed toward the goals of this life, and you will fail to find the path toward the future."

───◆◆◆───

Again, Khutön, Ngok, and Dromtönpa asked Atiśa, "Of all the teachings of the path, which is the best?" The master replied:

The best learning is realizing the truth of no-self.
The best discipline is taming your mindstream.
The best excellence is to have great altruism.
The best instruction is the constant observation of your mind.
The best antidote is the recognition that everything is devoid of intrinsic existence.
The best conduct is that which is at odds with the mundane world.
The best higher attainment is the lessening of your mental afflictions.
The best sign of higher attainment is a decrease in your attachment.
The best giving is the absence of possessiveness.
The best morality is a tranquil mind.
The best forbearance is to uphold humility.
The best joyful perseverance is to be able to let go of the endeavor.
The best concentration is the uncontrived mind.
The best wisdom is to make no identification of "I am" with anything.
The best spiritual teacher is to challenge your weaknesses.
The best instruction is to strike at your very own shortcomings.

The best friends are mindfulness and introspective
 awareness.
The best motivating factors are your enemies, obstacles,
 illnesses, and sufferings.
The best skillful means is to be free of second guesses.
The best beneficial deed is to help someone enter the
 Dharma.
The best help given is to turn someone's thoughts to
 the Dharma.

—— ∞ ——

Dromtönpa asked, "What is the most final among all teachings?"

"The most final among all teachings is the emptiness that is
endowed with the essence of compassion," Atiśa replied.

He continued, "For example, in the world there is a medicine
called 'the powerful single remedy' that counteracts all illnesses.
In the same manner, like the powerful single-remedy medicine,
if you realize the truth of emptiness, which is the nature of reality, this becomes an antidote against all affliction."

When asked, "If this is true, why have all those who claim
to have realized emptiness failed to minimize their attachment
and anger?" Atiśa replied:

"These people have arrived at mere, empty words, for if you
have genuinely realized the truth of emptiness, then your body,
speech, and mind are like a cotton cloth that has been [softened
by] pressing down under the feet or like barley soup into which
butter has been thrown for seasoning. Master Āryadeva states
that even if you develop a mere doubt as to whether the ultimate
mode of being of things is empty, this will shred cyclic existence
to pieces.[11] Therefore, if you have realized the truth of emptiness
without error, this is like [finding] the powerful single-remedy
medicine. Thus, all the teachings of the path are encompassed
within it."

———— ⟨∞⟩ ————

"How is that all the teachings of the path are encompassed within the realization of emptiness?" asked Dromtönpa.

Atiśa replied: "All the teachings of the path are embodied in the six perfections. And if practitioners realize the truth of emptiness without error, they will be free of deep desire and grasping attachment; hence, there is the uninterrupted perfection of giving. Since those who are free of grasping and attachment are not soiled by the stains of nonvirtue, there is the uninterrupted perfection of ethical discipline. Since they are devoid of anger from grasping at 'I am' and 'mine,' there is the uninterrupted perfection of forbearance. Since they are endowed with joy at the truth that has been realized, there is the uninterrupted perfection of joyful perseverance. Since they are free of distractions grasping at phenomena as substantially real, there is the uninterrupted perfection of concentration. Since they are free of conceiving anything in terms of the three spheres,[12] there is the uninterrupted perfection of wisdom."

———— ⟨∞⟩ ————

"If this is so, for one who has realized the truth, is it through the view of emptiness and its meditation alone that one becomes fully enlightened?" asked Dromtönpa.

The master replied, "There is nothing in this world of appearance and everyday convention that does not come into being except from one's own mind. The mind, too, is an empty awareness, and recognition of it [i.e., the empty mind] as the nonduality of awareness and emptiness is the *view*. Abiding in this continuously with mindfulness, free of distraction, is *meditation*. Gathering the two accumulations in an illusion-like manner from within such a state is *action*. When one can accomplish this in one's immediate experience through one's practice, it will become possible in dreams as well. When this becomes possible during dreams, it will then be possible at the time of death. When this becomes possible at the point of death, it will then become possible during the intermediate state as well. And when this happens during the intermediate state, one is certain to achieve the supreme attainment."

⸺⸺

Once when Master Atiśa was residing at Nyethang, the three teachers Shang Nachung Tönpa, Gyura Tönpa, and Lhetsang Tönpa asked him about the tenets of the epistemological schools.

Atiśa said: "There are many philosophical systems of both non-Buddhist and Buddhist schools, all of which are but garlands of conceptualization. Conceptualizations are beyond calculation and they have no use. As there is no time to spare in life, now is the time to seek what is most essential."

Shang Nachung Tönpa then asked, "How does one seek what is most essential?"

Atiśa replied: "Train your mind to cultivate loving-kindness and compassion toward all sentient beings, who equal the expanse of space. For their sake, strive to gather the two accumulations and dedicate all roots of virtue that arise from this toward the full enlightenment of all sentient beings. Make sure that you recognize the nature of all of these as empty and their characteristics as like dreams and illusions."

⸺⸺

When Master Atiśa first visited Ngari, he lived there for two years. There he gave many essential instructions to those headed by Lha Jangchup Ö.[13] He was intending to return to India, and as he was about to take to the road, Lha Jangchup Ö once again requested personal advice. When Atiśa responded that what had already been given in the past should suffice, Lha persisted with his plea. The master then gave the following instruction:

Emaho!

O friend, you whose knowledge is high and whose mind is
utterly clear,
though it is inappropriate for me, one of low intelligence
and lacking in accomplishments, to offer any advice,
as you, my excellent friend who is so dear to my heart, have
exhorted me,
I, a childlike one with small intelligence, offer this suggestion to your heart, my friend.

As one requires a teacher until the attainment of enlightenment, rely on a sublime teacher, O friend.
As one requires learning until the ultimate mode of being is
realized, listen to your teacher's essential instructions.
As the mere knowledge of the teachings does not lead to
full enlightenment, put it into practice, for knowing
alone is inadequate.
Distance yourself from those objects that afflict your mind,
and always reside in places that increase virtue.

As distractions cause harm, until one has attained stability,
seek solitary forests.
Forsake friends who give rise to affliction, seek those who
enhance virtue, and respect their wishes.
As there is no end to mundane chores, discard them and
abide with natural ease.
Throughout day and night dedicate your virtues and always
guard your mind.

As you've received essential instructions, whatever you
   do, meditation or otherwise, do so according to your
   teacher's words.

If you pursue this with great respect, you will reap its fruits
   before long.
If you act in accord with the Dharma from your heart, both
   provisions and support will be attained as byproducts.
O friends, sensual desires are insatiable, like drinking salt
   water; therefore cultivate contentment.

Despise all thoughts of haughtiness, conceit, and arrogance;
   be tranquil and tamed.
As distracting pursuits referred to as "merit" are obstacles to
   Dharma practice, relinquish them.
As offerings and honor are Māra's[14] lasso, measure them
   carefully like the weights of a scale.
As words of praise and fame are tricksters, expel them like
   spit or snot.

Though today happiness, good fortune, and friends may
   have converged, since this is only momentary, leave them
   behind.
Since the future is longer than the present, hide well your
   resources in treasure as provisions for the future.
As you must depart by leaving everything behind, there is
   no use for anything, so cling to nothing.
Cultivate compassion toward the weak; abandon mocking
   and disparaging them.

Have no prejudice of clinging to or recoiling from the
   classes of friends and enemies.
Have no jealousy toward the learned ones, but respect them
   and receive knowledge from them.

Do not scrutinize others' faults, but probe your own and
discard them like poisoned blood.

Think not of your virtues but of others'; like a servant, show
respect for all.

Cultivate recognition of all beings as your parents and love
them as if they were your own children.

With a smiling face and loving heart, always speak what is
true without hostility.

Since excessive pointless conversation causes confusion,
engage in appropriate measures of speech.

Since excessive pointless chores disrupt your virtuous deeds,
discard non-Dharma pursuits.

Do not strive too much in meaningless pursuits, for this is
wasteful hardship.

Come what may, do not die with attachment; since the
other shore is born of karma, it is better to rest your
mind at ease.

Alas! If you become despised by the sublime beings, you are
as good as dead; so be honest, not deceitful.

Since the sufferings of this life arise from past karma, do not
blame others.

Since all happiness is the teachers' blessings, repay their
kindness.

Since you cannot tame others' minds while your own mind
remains untamed, first discipline your own mind.

Since you cannot help enhance others if you lack superior
cognition, strive well in your meditative practice.

Since you are certain to leave your accumulated wealth
behind when you depart, commit no negative act for
its sake.

Since this wealth of distractions is without essence, give
   charity graced with gifts.
Since it beautifies this life and leads to happiness in the
   future, always observe pure ethical discipline.
Since hatred proliferates in the degenerate age, don the
   armor of forbearance free of anger.
Since in indolence you might be left behind, ignite the
   flame of joyful perseverance like a blazing fire.

Since it is on the road of distraction that one exhausts
   one's lifespan, the time has now come to endeavor in
   concentration.
Since it is due to wrong views that one fails to realize the
   ultimate mode of being, inspect well the perfect truth.
O friends, there is no joy in this mire of samsara, so depart
   to liberation's dry shores.
Practice well the teachers' instructions and drain the lake of
   samsara's suffering.

Keep this advice well in your hearts and listen to this suggestion, for this is not mere mouthing of words.
If you do this, I'll be happy, and both you and others will
   enjoy happiness.
Listen well, dear friend, to these words of advice from an
   ignorant man.

Thus the master Atiśa, the sole lord, advised Lhatsün Jangchup Ö.

———— ❀❀ ————

Once when Atiśa was residing in the rocky mountains of Yerpa,
he gave the following instruction to Ölgöpa Yeshé Bar:[15]

Homage to blessed Ārya Tārā! Homage to the sublime teachers! O noble son, reflect well on these words of mine.

In general, the lifespan of human beings in this degenerate age is short, and there are a great many fields of knowledge one could pursue. As you have no certainty how long you will live, seek to accomplish swiftly your greatest aspirations.

Do not say "I am a fully ordained monk" while busying yourself with activities of mundane livelihood, such as acquiring possessions.

Do not say "I am a hermit monk" while nursing the pain of having your mundane pursuits undermined—or the fear of this happening—even though you are residing in the wilderness.

Do not say "I am a hermit monk" while your mind remains engrossed in admiration of this life's sensual pleasures and in harmful intentions.

Do not say "I am a hermit monk" while not relinquishing association with the worldly even though you are residing in the wilderness, or while continuing to pass time in frivolous chatter, or in conversations related to a householder's life, with whoever happens to be around.

Do not say "I am a bodhisattva monk" while being incapable of tolerating even the slightest of harms to yourself or rendering the slightest of benefits to others.

If you continue to say as much, despite such actions, you are telling a great lie to the world. You might be able to make such claims to the world, but you cannot deceive those who possess the divine eye, unobstructed at all times. Second, you should not make such claims because the law of karma and its effects follows after you. Third, you should not do so to beings who possess the eye of the Dharma. Furthermore, you must recall your pledges in the presence of the meditation deities and the teachers when you generated the awakening mind.

When you encounter things that try your patience, do not become despondent or exclaim, "O this is so difficult!" and fail to practice forbearance. Remember: though this may be difficult, you have no choice but to face it. Hesitation born of wondering whether something is too difficult is relevant only to the period prior to taking the vows and making the pledge. After you have taken the vows and made the pledge, if you undermine them, this constitutes deceiving the meditation deities and teachers. Therefore, even when it is difficult, remember the only choice is to practice forbearance.

Also, the point of residing in the wilderness is to forsake association with the worldly and to stop clinging to friends and family. Relinquishing these ensures the cessation of all causes and conditions for distraction and conceptualization, such as yearning for sensual objects. You look only at the precious mind of awakening and never, even for a single instant, pursue the thought that worries about mundane pursuits.

Mundane conceptions arise frequently and remain powerful because of failing to engage correctly in the practice of Dharma in the past and because of a weak mental habit for such practice. Therefore, if you fail to apply special antidotes against them, residing in the wilderness will be pointless, for then you will only be like the birds and wild animals that live there. Do not think that since it is too difficult at present you will engage in the practice later on; if a blind person loses hold of a precious jewel, he will not find it again.

When you undertake the practice, do not measure in terms of years and months; rather, analyzing your mind, assess your level of realization by how deeply you are habituated to the practice. Ask whether your afflictions are diminished. Constantly watch your mind. Do not inflict suffering upon yourself; do not deceive yourself; do not deceive the meditation deities and the teachers; and do not do things that spell doom for both self and others.

Even if the mundane goals of this life are undermined, [this is good, for] that which must be undermined is becoming so. Say you are faced with a pile of waste that you have to sweep up and throw away. If someone were there to help you, wouldn't you be delighted? In the same way, whatever conceptualizations you have about the affairs of this life must be relinquished with all available antidotes, and if your teachers and special friends help you do this, aren't you delighted?

Having pledged in the presence of your meditation deities and teachers, do not discriminate among the objects of your giving. Although differences do exist among the objects, as far as training in the awakening mind is concerned, there is no difference among them.

Do not be angry toward those who inflict harm, for if you get angry with those who cause harm, when will you practice forbearance? Whenever afflictions arise you must remember their antidotes. What point is a Dharma practice that allows afflictions to roam free? So when looking at the precious awakening mind, do it without giving a single opening to loss of mindfulness. For when a gap is opened due to lapsed mindfulness, the māras of affliction will enter, and if they do they will create obstacles for the awakening mind. When this happens remember that it will undermine others' welfare, and there will be no choice for you either but birth in the lower realms. Though you may have the thought, "But I have practiced Dharma," this will mean nothing, and you will go empty-handed.

O noble son, when at last you die, be sure you do not cause your teachers and special friends sorrow and disappointment. Do not cause laypeople who respect the Dharma to become disappointed and doubt-ridden.

If you do not examine again and again by comparing your own mind with the sacred scriptures, though you might feel, "I have practiced Dharma," the practice and the person will remain far apart. And if, when you die, instead of experiencing the signs of having trained your mind in the awakening mind, you experience the signs of the lower realms, others will have no option but to feel disappointment and sorrow. Therefore, giving up entirely practice tainted with the vain thought "I have spent my entire life in Dharma practice," ensure that you do not enter death's door empty-handed.

In brief, even if you reside in the wilderness, if you have not let go of mundane pursuits and do not avert your mind from yearning for sensual objects, then the Dharma has failed to benefit you. This is called "not having accomplished one's task." If you hope to conduct yourself in such a way that both this life and future lives are not undermined, then Dharma practice has become a mere hobby for you. Such a hobby will remain nothing but a Dharma practice of words, food, and pretense.

Therefore, rely on special friends; do not associate with negative companions; do not reside in fixed locations; and do not stay at one place and hoard contaminated possessions. Whatever you do, do so by relating it to the Dharma. Ensure that whatever you do becomes an antidote to the afflictions. When you conduct yourself in this manner, it becomes perfect Dharma practice, so put effort into this. If higher qualities arise in you, do not become inflated with conceit, for you will fall prey to Māra.

While residing in places on the margins of town, ensure that you yourself are pacified and tamed. Be modest in desires and learn to be content. Do not focus on your own good qualities or seek out others' shortcomings. Do not be afraid and apprehensive. Do not have too many preconceptions. Cultivate a good heart. Do not be distracted by misguided ways but contemplate the Dharma on a regular basis. Adopt humility, accept losses, give up trumpeting your good deeds, let go of deep desires, cultivate affection, and have moderation in all things. Be easy to please and easy to nurture. Run away from the worldly like a wild animal.

If you do not relinquish mundane norms, you are not a Dharma practitioner. If you do not relinquish the four pursuits, such as farming, you are not a monk.[16] If you do not discard sensual objects, you are not a fully ordained monk. If you lack loving-kindness and the awakening mind, you are not a bodhisattva. If you do not let go of mundane pursuits, you are not a meditating yogi.

Be not a servant to sensual desires. In brief, while residing in the wilderness, have few chores and undertake only the practice of Dharma. In this way ensure that when death approaches you will have no regrets.

Again, Atiśa said:

Now in this age of degeneration is not the time for bravado;
　　it is the time to lay bare the bones of your heart.[17]
Now is not the time to claim the high ground; it is the
　　time to stake the ground of humility.
Now is not the time to seek an entourage and servants;
　　it is the time to seek solitude.
Now is not the time to measure your students; it is
　　the time to measure yourself.
Now is not the time to cling to words; it is the time to
　　contemplate their meaning.
Now is not the time to travel around; it is the time
　　to remain settled in one place.

2. The Sayings of Dromtönpa

Known also simply as Drom, Dromtönpa's personal name is Gyalwai Jungné. He is considered a cofounder of the Kadam tradition along with Atiśa, of whom he is the spiritual heir. When he was young, Drom met a master from eastern Tibet named Setsün, who was on his way to Nepal and India. Following Setsün's return to Tibet, Dromtönpa became his student and studied various Buddhist texts and practices under him. Around this time Dromtönpa also began a serious study of Sanskrit with an Indian paṇḍita, possibly the famed Smṛti Jñānakīrti. Thus by the time Dromtönpa met with Atiśa, he was already an accomplished scholar with a good command of Sanskrit.

Of course Dromtönpa's meeting with Master Atiśa marked the turning point of his spiritual career. The success of Atiśa's mission, especially in central Tibet, was due in large part to Dromtönpa. It was Drom who first gathered together the great and greatest in the Tibetan Buddhist world of the time to meet the Indian master. It was Drom who largely dictated the style of teachings given by Atiśa in central Tibet—placing emphasis on such basics as the law of karma; stressing the maintenance of sound ethical discipline; developing a systematic, graduated approach to the path to enlightenment; and, most of all, unwaveringly advocating the cultivation of an altruistic awakening mind rooted in universal compassion—all of which became hallmarks of the Kadam tradition. It was also Drom who, through the founding of Radreng Monastery, ensured the long-term continuation of Master Atiśa's legacy in Tibet. It was Drom who preserved a detailed timeline of Atiśa's years in Tibet, thus providing the basis for all subsequent biographies of the master. Finally, Drom collaborated with Atiśa on various projects, translating important Sanskrit Buddhist texts into Tibetan.

The portrait of Drom that emerges from his various biographies is of a deeply humble and truly compassionate man. On a personal level Drom chose to remain a lay practitioner, not taking the full monastic ordination so that he would have one less ground for status-related self-importance. He also advised his disciples, "Even if you are being honored by others with their heads bowed to you, on your part you should remain humble." Drom was particularly struck by the suffering of people afflicted with the debilitating illness of leprosy, which seems to have been not uncommon in certain regions of central Tibet during his time. It is said that at one point Drom actually helped nurse some lepers himself. Thanks largely to the influence of the *Book of Kadam*, the core of which is attributed to Master Atiśa, Dromtönpa over time came to be closely identified with Avalokiteśvara, the buddha of compassion believed by Tibetans to have a special destiny with the Land of Snows. Drom's disciples included, among others, the three Kadam brothers—Potowa, Chengawa, and Phuchungwa—Master Gönpawa, and Khamlungpa.[18]

The three brothers, disciples of the spiritual mentor Dromtönpa, requested of him a method to condense the essential points of all the aspects of the path to omniscience.

Dromtönpa stated: "For an individual practitioner to attain the buddhahood of omniscience, an inconceivable number of precepts can be entries to the path. As for what is to be cultivated within, however, there is only one thing. What is this single point? It is emptiness endowed with the essence of compassion.

"To specify its aspects further, *empty* refers to the ultimate awakening mind; it is the ultimate mode of being of all phenomena realized as primordially unborn. *Compassion* is the conventional awakening mind, which is the generation of great compassion toward those sentient beings who have failed to realize this [unborn nature]. Therefore Mahayana practitioners for whom the two awakening minds have not yet arisen should first strive to generate them. In the middle, while training in the two awakening minds that have already arisen in their mental continua, they gain certainty that they will actualize their ultimate results—the Buddha's truth body and form body.

"Although there are many methods for generating the awakening mind where it has not yet arisen, when summarized for practice there are only three root methods and their nine principal branches. First, the three roots are subsumed into (1) training the mind, (2) gathering the accumulations, and (3) seeking the meditative absorptions.

"Their nine principal branches are: First, although there exist numerous methods for training the mind, the three principal ones are: (1) meditation on impermanence, (2) cultivation of loving-kindness and compassion, and (3) meditation on the two selflessnesses. Among the methods for training the mind, these three are the greatest, and these three, moreover, encompass all other methods.

"Although there are numerous methods for gathering the accumulations, the three principal ones are: (1) making offerings of material things and service to the teachers, (2) making offerings to the Three Jewels, and (3) making offerings of material things and service to the spiritual community. Among the methods of accumulating merit, these three are the greatest, and they also encompass all other methods.

"Although there are numerous ways of seeking meditative absorption, the three principal ones are: (1) observing pure ethical discipline, (2) making supplications to the lineage teachers, and (3) seeking both physical and mental solitude. These three alone are the greatest, and they encompass the methods for seeking the meditative absorptions of tranquil abiding (*śamatha*) and insight (*vipaśyanā*).

"Thus, as a result of practicing these nine points in an integrated way, the two awakening minds arise in your mental continuum with spontaneous force. The moment the ultimate awakening mind arises, the realization of all external and internal phenomena as free of dualistic elaborations—as empty and unborn—will spontaneously arise as well. At that time you will have found within yourself a joyful state of mind. The moment the conventional awakening mind arises, feelings especially of loving-kindness and compassion toward the sentient beings who have failed to recognize this [truth of emptiness] will arise. Your sole task in life will become working for the welfare of sentient beings. At that point whatever activities you engage in will become beneficial to other sentient beings.

"You will thus combine these two awakening minds into a union so that at the very moment [when the realization of] emptiness [is present], compassion for sentient beings especially will grow, while at the very moment of compassion, you will not observe a substantial reality of oneself and other sentient beings. Thus by recognizing all appearances as empty and like illusions, when these two minds arise in union, you have entered the unmistaken path of the Great Vehicle. As you become trained in this union, and when your habituation to it becomes perfected, you will attain the perfect truth body and the perfect form body. From the ultimate awakening mind you attain the truth body, while from the conventional awakening mind—i.e., compassion—you attain the form body. And from mastery of the indivisible union of these two you attain the indivisible nature of the truth and form bodies."

Again, the three brothers asked Dromtönpa, "Of the two—view and action—which is more important for the perfection of one's own interests and others' welfare?"

Dromtönpa replied, "In order to perfect the welfare of self and others after entering the door of the Great Vehicle, you need to combine perfect view and perfect action. One in isolation from the other cannot accomplish this aim."

"What then constitutes perfect view and perfect action?" they asked.

Dromtönpa responded: "*Perfect view* refers to the recognition that all phenomena are, from the point of view of their ultimate nature, devoid of existing in any substantial mode of reality and free of all extremes of eternalism and nihilism, and the recognition that all external and internal phenomena are, from the conventional perspective, like dreams, illusions, and apparitions. You recognize them simply as expressions of your own mind, and you thus never place your trust in anything or chase after any objects.

"*Perfect action* refers to respecting the law of karma and its effects—understanding that on the dream-like, illusion-like level of conventional truth, the positive and negative karmas do not fail to give rise to their effects. Out of great compassion you strive for the welfare of the sentient beings who fail to recognize this truth.

"Such perfect view and perfect action arise naturally for someone in whom the two awakening minds have arisen."

"If this is so, what flaws arise when view and action are in isolation from each other?" they asked.

Dromtönpa replied, "If you do not respect the law of karma and its effects and let your behavior become degraded, you will be incapable of working for the welfare of both self and others, so your view will also become misguided. If you possess perfect action but fail to realize the ultimate mode of being, you will be incapable of working for the welfare of both self and others, so your conduct will become misguided. Therefore, if you do not combine view and action, you will fall into error; you must train in their union."

—∞∞∞—

Again, the three brothers asked Dromtönpa, "Of the two—practicing in solitude and benefiting other sentient beings through teaching—which has a greater impact?"

Dromtönpa replied: "If a beginner without the slightest experience of realization within his or her mental continuum were to help others through teaching, it would have no benefit. It would be like pouring blessings from an empty container: there will be no blessings to pour out. The essential instructions [of such a teacher] would be like beer made of fermented grains that have not been crushed well: such essential instructions will have no taste or vitality.

"A person who has attained the stage of 'heat'[19] but not its stability will not be able to bring about the welfare of other sentient beings, for it would be like pouring blessings from a full container: when the other container becomes full, it itself would become empty. The essential instructions of such a person would be like passing a torch from one hand to another: when the other hand is illuminated, one's own would become darkened.

"Once one has attained the bodhisattva levels, one should engage in the activities of bringing about the welfare of sentient beings as much as possible. Here the blessings are like the higher attainments flowing from an excellent vase: even when all others are enhanced, it never becomes empty. The essential instructions of such a person resemble a source lamp: even when all other lamps are lighted, the source lamp itself does not become obscured.

"Therefore, during this age of degeneration is the time for ordinary beings to familiarize their minds with loving-kindness and compassion in solitude. It is not the time to actually benefit sentient beings. It is the time to guard against the afflictions within your mind. This is analogous to the period when it is more appropriate to guard the fledgling shoot of a medicinal tree than to cut it."

⸺⸺

Once a teacher from Kham asked Dromtönpa about the meaning of the two selflessnesses.

Dromtönpa replied, "If you were to probe with your mind and search from the top of your crown aperture to the bottom of the soles of your feet, not a single entity would you find that is called the 'self.' That nonfinding is the selflessness of persons. Recognizing that the searching mind, too, is devoid of intrinsic existence is the selflessness of phenomena."

⸺⸺

A woman named Salo Tsomo of Drom from the Tré region of Phenpo made an offering of forty bags of barley [to Dromtönpa] and asked the following question: "My brother Dromtsik sent me to give you a message, O spiritual mentor. All the monks here have gathered in order to attain the omniscient state of buddhahood. We two siblings seek the same attainment. Spiritual mentor, since you possess the essential instructions of Master Atiśa, the sole lord, as if poured from one full vase into another, today we request that you confer on us, keeping nothing hidden, the essential instructions for attaining buddhahood."

The spiritual mentor Dromtönpa replied, "First extensively contemplate death and impermanence and the law of karma and its effects, and guard the purity of all the vows that you have pledged to observe. Cultivate loving-kindness and compassion extensively and stabilize the awakening mind. To this end, gather the two accumulations by means of various methods. Purify negative karmas through various means. While maintaining the nonobjectification of the three spheres[20] with regard to all phenomena, dedicate all your roots of virtue toward the attainment of full enlightenment by all sentient beings. If you conduct yourself in this way, you need feel no sorrow for not having met Atiśa. There is no greater teaching than this for becoming fully awakened. In the future none need feel saddened for not having met me, the old man of Drom, for there is no greater teachings than this."

Once a lay practitioner asked the spiritual mentor Dromtönpa, "If one remains undivorced from loving-kindness, compassion, and the awakening mind, is this not always the cause, directly or indirectly, for the fulfillment of others' welfare?"

Dromtönpa replied: "Without question this is the cause for the perfect realization of others' welfare. This will become the cause for the perfect realization of your own welfare as well, for if you remain undivorced from loving-kindness, compassion, and the awakening mind, it is impossible to be reborn in the three lower realms of existence. Starting right now you can become an 'irreversible' person. If, however, due to past grave negative karmas and powerful adverse current conditions, you were to take birth in the lower realms, a mere single instance of recollecting loving-kindness, compassion, and the awakening mind would, that very instant, free you from that lower-realm birth. You would be certain to achieve the status of an extraordinary human or celestial existence. For example, the *Guide to the Bodhisattva's Way of Life* states:

> Whatever suffering is in the world
> arises from wishing for one's own happiness;

whatever happiness is in the world
arises from wishing for others' happiness.

What need is there to say more?
The childish pursue their own interests,
while the buddhas act for the welfare of others;
observe the difference between these two.[21]

"Therefore, it has been taught that loving-kindness, compassion, and the awakening mind are the causes for accomplishing the great purposes of both oneself and others."

Again, an elder was once circumambulating the outer perimeter at Radreng Monastery. Dromtönpa asked him, "O elder, performing circumambulation may be satisfying, but wouldn't it be better if you practiced the Dharma?"

The elder felt that, instead of performing circumambulations, perhaps it would be more effective if he were to read Mahayana sutras, so he began to read sutras on the temple veranda. Dromtönpa then asked him, "Reading sutras might also be satisfying, but wouldn't it be better if you practiced the Dharma?"

The elder took this as a sign that, when contrasted with reading sutras, engaging in meditative absorption is more profitable, so he abandoned reading sutras and sat down with his eyes closed. Again, Dromtönpa asked, "Meditating might also be satisfying, but wouldn't it be better to practice the Dharma instead?"

Failing to think of any other method, the elder asked, "O spiritual mentor, then what kind of Dharma practice would you have me undertake?"

It is said that Drom replied, "O elder, give up this life; give up this life."

In this way Dromtönpa stated that so long as we fail to forsake attachment to this life, whatever we undertake does not become Dharma practice, for such an act remains within the bounds of the eight mundane concerns. By contrast, if we let go of attachment to this life, we will remain untainted by the eight mundane concerns. Only then will whatever we do become a path to liberation.

Once Potowa asked the spiritual mentor Dromtönpa, "What is the demarcation between Dharma and non-Dharma?"

Dromtönpa replied, "If it is a remedy against affliction, it is Dharma; if not, it is not Dharma. If it is at variance with all worldly people, it is Dharma; if it is in accord with the worldly, it is not Dharma. If its trace is positive, it is Dharma; if not, it is not Dharma."

3. The Sayings of Other Early Kadam Masters

GÖNPAWA (1016–82)

Gönpawa, whose personal name was Wangchuk Gyaltsen, was a prominent student of both Master Atiśa and Dromtönpa. Following the death of Naljorpa, who succeeded Dromtönpa as the head of Radreng Monastery, Gönpawa assumed the abbotship of the monastery for five years.

Born in Kham in the eastern part of Tibet, Gönpawa as a young man heard one day from a group of traveling merchants that an important Indian teacher had arrived in western Tibet. He is said to have immediately joined a group of merchants traveling to central Tibet. With no provisions to support himself on the road, Gönpawa trekked across the Tibetan plateau begging along the way. Gönpawa's younger sister, upon learning of his journey, is reported to have exclaimed, "It is sad enough to discover that my brother has gone to central Tibet. What is more disheartening, though, is to learn that he went the entire way as a beggar." After meeting Master Atiśa, Gönpawa never turned back, remaining steadfast in his pursuit of instructions from the master and engaging in meditation practice. Among Master Atiśa's numerous students Gönpawa came to be particularly famed for his single-pointed diligence in meditation practice and for being an expert counselor to those who sought help in dealing with adversity arisen from serious meditation practice. In fact, Gönpawa is said to have once joked, "Dromtönpa served the master as his interpreter; Naljorpa served him as his attendant; if you are here for meditation instructions, you should come to me."

Gönpawa's students included Neusurpa, Kharak Gomchung, and Shawo Gangpa, all well-known early masters of the Kadam tradition.[22]

The spiritual mentor Gönpawa said:

The root of omniscience lies in the two accumulations [of wisdom and merit].

The root of the two accumulations lies in the awakening mind.

The root of the awakening mind lies in loving-kindness and compassion.

The root of the precepts of all of these practices lies in the six perfections.

The root of giving lies in the absence of grasping attachment.

The root of ethical discipline lies in reliance on good companions.

The root of forbearance lies in upholding humility.

The root of joyful perseverance lies in contemplating death.

The root of concentration lies in seeking solitude.

The root of wisdom lies in observing your own mind.

The root of blessings lies in admiration and respect.

The root of higher attainments lies in the vows and commitments.

The root of higher qualities lies in learning, reflection, and meditation.

The root of others' welfare lies in the absence of selfish desires.

And the root of both self and others' welfare lies in meditative practice.

Yerpa Shangtsün (eleventh century)

Yerpa Shangtsün, whose personal name was Yeshé Bar, was a senior student of Master Atiśa known particularly for his profound realization and embodiment of the truth of impermanence. Never attached to whatever meager things he happened to possess, Yerpa Shangtün viewed them not as belonging to himself but as being held temporarily so as to give them to someone who needed them more. Contemplation of death was such a constant for him that he perceived every event as illustrating the fundamental truth of impermanence. For example, when he felt ill, Yerpa would immediately remark that this is a message from impermanence warning him of the inevitable truth of his mortality. The famed Kadam master Potowa, a disciple of Yerpa, is said to have remarked: "It's our master Yerpa Shangtsün who has actualized within true awareness of death. Contemplating death constantly, he does nothing but engage in Dharma practice. On our part, we should emulate his example as much as we can."[23]

Yerpa Shangtsünpa said: "If from the depths of our heart we aspire for liberation, we must abide in the four natural attributes of a noble one in both our thoughts and actions while continually contemplating death and impermanence.

"The four natural attributes of a noble one are: (1) being content with modest clothing, (2) being content with modest food, (3) being content with modest bedding, and (4) being content with modest facilities for subsistence, such as medicine for illness. Alternatively, they are: (1) being modest in one's desires, (2) having the ability to be content, (3) being easy to nurture, and (4) being easy to fulfill.

"*Being modest in one's desires* refers to not having a deep desire for excellent facilities and for abundance, and to giving up

49

all material possessions. *Having the ability to be content* refers to being content with few and modest material things. *Being easy to nurture* refers to being able to subsist on modest clothing, bedding, and food. *Being easy to fulfill* refers to being satisfied with minimal and modest offerings, material gifts, and services.

"Since all the factors of enlightenment reside in the mindstream of a person who abides in the four natural attributes of a noble one, they are known as 'abiding in the four natural attributes of a noble one.' As all negative karmas—the causes of cyclic existence and the lower realms of existence—reside in the mindstreams of those who are motivated by the mundane desires of this life and who thus do not abide in the four natural attributes of a noble one, they are known as 'abiding in the natural attributes of Māra.' If we fail to relinquish desire in this life, we will therefore fall prey to the power of desire in our future lives as well, so we must relinquish all mundane desires pertaining to this life and abide in the four natural attributes of a noble one. To relinquish mundane desires of this life, it is critical to constantly meditate on impermanence, which is their antidote. For if you fail to meditate on impermanence one morning, by midday you will have become someone who is concerned with the mundane affairs of this life."

———————

Again, Yerpa Shangtsün said: "If you aspire to attain omniscient buddhahood, you need three untainted factors: (1) your virtues must not be tainted by mundane considerations about this life, (2) your actions of body and speech must not be tainted by the afflictions, and (3) your meditative practice must not be tainted by the mindset of the self-enlightened ones. In brief, your action must illustrate perfect realization.

"What is a measure gaining perfect realization? You are flexible when you need to be, so your view must be flexible. You are strict when you need to be, so your conduct must be strict. You are heroic when you need to be, so you must be heroic in applying antidotes to the afflictions. You are humble when you need to be, so you must have humility borne of forbearance when facing provocation and so on from others."

Potowa (1027–1105)

Potowa, whose personal name was Rinchen Sal, was one of the "three Kadam brothers" who were the principal students of Master Dromtönpa. At a young age Potowa joined the monastic order at Yerpa, where he also met with Master Atiśa. There he received, with help from Naktso as the interpreter, a teaching on Kamalaśila's *Stages of Meditation.* When Drom was dying, his head lying on Potowa's lap, the latter's sadness caused a few teardrops to fall on Drom's clothes. Potowa asked, "After you're no more, to whom can we turn as our teacher?" In response Drom advised, "From now on seek your spiritual teacher in the scriptures. Be kindhearted and you will definitely meet someone special." Over time Potowa came to be a great master of the Kadam tradition in his own right and is perhaps the most celebrated Kadam master after the two founding fathers, Atiśa and Dromtönpa.

Much of what we know about Potowa is based on accounts of his life related by his immediate disciples, including a biography of the master in verse composed by Lang Jarawa. The picture that emerges from these accounts is of a master who was revered as a *mahāsthavira*, a great monastic elder whose contributions to the Dharma were extensive. He was versed in the scriptures, highly learned, meticulous in his observance of monastic precepts, and lived a life of true nonattachment and altruism. Potowa is said to have remarked, "Ever since I can remember, I have always felt saddened by other's pain and have instinctively sought ways to help remove that suffering. And when I saw others happy, I always felt joyful and would think of how that happiness could be sustained. So when others were happy, I felt joyful; when others suffered, I felt saddened. Even when I saw two people walking together, I would wish for them to have their friendship last for a long time." Potowa thus appeared to have a naturally compassionate disposition, which later came to be developed to its highest potential through the teachings of the Kadam tradition.

After Dromtönpa's death, Potowa held the abbotship of Radreng

Monastery (after Naljorpa and Gönpawa). During his abbotship of Radreng, Potowa established the tradition of taking Atiśa's *Lamp for the Path to Enlightenment* as the principal text of practice and complementing it with six other Indian Buddhist texts: Śāntideva's (1) *Compendium of Trainings* and (2) *Guide to the Bodhisattva's Way of Life;* Maitreya's (3) *Ornament of Mahayana Sutras;* Asaṅga's (4) *Bodhisattva Levels;* Āryaśūra's (5) *Garland of Birth Stories;* and (6) the *Collections of Aphorisms,* attributed to the Buddha. These six texts came to be known as "*the six treatises of the Kadam school.*" Over time Potowa came to be recognized as the founder of one of the three major lineages of the Kadam tradition, namely "the Kadam lineage of treatises."

Two important works by Potowa survive. One is a short mind-training text posthumously entitled *Potowa's Long Chat;* the other is a root text on the stages of the path (*lamrim*) instruction entitled *Teachings through Similes.* This second text is the focus of a major commentarial work by Master Chegom, editor of our present text. Another independent work on *lamrim* emerged on the basis of Potowa's teachings, entitled the *Blue Compendium,* which was revered especially by the great Tsongkhapa, who remarked, "If you are a spiritual teacher, you cannot remain ignorant of the *Blue Compendium.*"[24] Compiled by Potowa's student Dölpa Sherap Gyatso, the *Blue Compendium* is a remarkable work in verse presenting the entire stages of the path to enlightenment. Included among Potowa's disciples are such luminaries of the Kadam school as Dölpa Sherap Gyatso, Langri Thangpa (author of the famed *Eight Verses of Mind Training*), Sharawa, and Drakarwa.[25]

───────

Once the spiritual mentor Potowa was asked by a lay practitioner, "To engage in a single-pointed practice of Dharma, what is most important?"

Potowa replied: "To engage in a single-pointed practice of Dharma, contemplation of impermanence is most important. For if you contemplate death and impermanence: in the beginning, it will *cause* you to enter Dharma; in the middle, it will act as a *condition* motivating you to engage in virtuous actions; and finally, it will act as a *factor* to realizing perfect equanimity with regard to the ultimate nature of reality.

"Again, if you contemplate impermanence: in the beginning, it will act as a *cause* for enabling you to let go of attachment to this life; in the middle, it will act as a *condition* for giving up clinging to all aspects of cyclic existence; and finally, it will act as a *factor* for entering the path to nirvana.

"Again, if you contemplate impermanence and its realization arises in your mind: in the beginning, it will act as a *cause* for faith to arise; in the middle, it will serve as a *condition* to inspire joyful perseverance; and finally, it will be a *factor* giving rise to wisdom.

"Again, if you contemplate impermanence and its realization arises in your mind: in the beginning, it will act as a *cause* for inspiring armor-like joyous effort; in the middle, it will act as a *condition* to inspire the joyous effort of actual application; and finally, it will act as a *factor* to inspire irreversible joyful perseverance."

Once Kyangtsa Dortsül asked the spiritual mentor Potowa for an instruction. Potowa replied:

"Contemplate impermanence repeatedly, and when the thought that death is inevitable arises there will be no hardship in abandoning negative karma and engaging in virtue.

"In addition, repeatedly cultivate loving-kindness and compassion, and when they arise in your mental continuum, there will no longer be any hardship in working for the welfare of sentient beings.

"In addition, repeatedly meditate on emptiness, which is the ultimate mode of being of all phenomena. And when this realization arises in your mental continuum, there will no longer be any hardship in eliminating delusion."

———∞———

Again, Potowa generally gave the following teaching to the assembly of his disciples:

"In general, the blessed Buddha, taking into account the existence of the eighty-four thousand classes of sentient beings or categories of afflictions, taught, as antidotes to these, eighty-four heaps of teachings. All of these teachings, when condensed in words, are encompassed within the three precious baskets of scripture. In terms of their subject matter, they are embodied in the three precious higher trainings.

"Of the three precious higher trainings, it is first on the basis of the higher training in morality that the higher training in meditation arises. On the basis of the higher training in meditation, the higher training in wisdom arises. This, then, eradicates the afflictions from their roots, thus leading to full awakening. Therefore, since the first of the three higher trainings—higher training in morality—is the foundation of the rest, beginners must take morality as their principal practice.

"Attachment is a factor that is contrary to morality. Indeed, attachment is at the root of every affliction, for it is on the basis of attachment that every affliction arises; through it, negative karma is accumulated and one wanders in cyclic existence. To eliminate attachment, its antidote—meditation on foulness—is taught.

"There are five different methods for this meditation on foulness.

1. The first, *visualizing the object as one's mother, as one's child, or as a sister*, is as follows: When the image of an object of attachment such as a woman becomes manifest and you experience

lustful attachment, if that woman is older than you, cultivate the thought of her as your mother. If you experience lustful attachment for a woman who is your own age, cultivate the thought of her as your sister. If you experience lustful attachment for a younger woman, cultivate the thought of her as your daughter. By meditating in these ways, your lustful attachment will be averted.

2. If, despite engaging in such meditations, your lustful attachment is not overcome, the second, *cultivating the factors of a sense of shame and consideration of others*, is as follows: Generate the thought, 'If I entertain such improper thoughts in my mind, the buddhas and bodhisattvas, who possess the wisdom eye of unobstructed sight, will come to know and see this. They will be displeased and I will not be protected. If I engage in unbecoming conduct, the gods of the earth and heavens will proclaim this to others; in this life my infamy will spread everywhere. In future lives, too, I will depart to the lower realms.' As you practice in this manner, bringing to mind a sense of shame and consideration of others at all stages, attachment will cease.

3. However, if despite such meditations your lustful attachment does not cease, there is, third, *visualizing the image of the object as being foul and foul smelling*. The first part of this, meditating on its foulness simultaneously, is as follows: Visualize the woman's body[26] as being a container of thirty-two foul substances and a city of eighty thousand classes of worms, just like the example of a dog's corpse, infested with maggots, lying rotten in the summer.

The gradual meditation is as follows: First, visualize the woman's body as being discolored, then as festering, then as bloated, as cut up, as infested with worms, as gnawed, and finally as a skeleton.[27] Through these visualizations, your attachment will cease.

4. However, if this also does not stop your attachment, the fourth, *meditating on the object as an enemy or a slayer*, is as follows: Reflect, 'This woman is my enemy, for she undermines thoughts that accord with Dharma practice.[28] She is the slayer of liberation's lifeline. She is a hailstorm destroying the harvest of positive karma. She is a thief that robs away all factors that lead to perfection. She is a demon that obstructs all roots of virtue. She is a prison guard that prevents me from escaping the suffering of cyclic existence. She is a troublemaker that gives impetus to every affliction. Like the furnace chamber of the hells, she is a source of all sufferings.' As you meditate on these, your lustful attachment will certainly come to cease.

5. The fifth, *visualizing the object as the trick of an illusion*, is as follows: Reflect, 'A magician, for example, tricks many people by conjuring numerous creatures, such as men, women, horses, and elephants, with most attractive appearances and features. Likewise, through their attachment and clinging to things, all of which are false, deceptive, and devoid of intrinsic existence like such illusions, sentient beings undergo suffering in the cycle of existence. In particular, this false, deceptive body of a woman, which is of little benefit and a source of enormous faults, has uninterruptedly deceived me at all times in the past, and it will do so today.' By meditating this way your lustful attachment will come to cease.

"If, despite meditating through all these methods, you fail to overcome attachment, the māras have entered your heart. Therefore you must seek to receive from your teacher some means of overcoming the māras."

CHENGAWA (1033–1103)

Chengawa Tsültrim Bar was the youngest of the "three Kadam brothers." At eighteen Chengawa joined the monastic order at Tölung. While there he visited Nyemo, where Master Atiśa was in residence, and attended a teaching on the awakening mind. It was during this teaching that Atiśa is said to have placed his right hand on Chengawa's head and predicted that he would be a great upholder of his lineage. From the age of twenty-five Chengawa became a close disciple of Dromtönpa, often serving him as a personal attendant. In fact, the name Chengawa means "one who remains in the presence."

In a visionary experience Chengawa met with the Indian master Nāgabodhi and received instructions from him, which he summarized into four sets of four practices. The set of four practices that is most well known is comprised of: (1) the yoga of recognizing all appearances as illusions by means of the analogy of sleep and dreams, (2) the yoga of recognizing the indivisibility of appearance and emptiness by means of the analogy of water and ice, (3) the yoga of recognizing all phenomena as being of a single taste by means of the analogy of the taste and mass of molasses, and (4) engaging in the conduct of the six perfections.

Chengawa founded the monastery of Lo, which housed around seven hundred residents by the end of his life. He is recognized as the founder of "the Kadam lineage of instructions," and his students included such luminaries as Jayülwa Shönu Ö, Tölungpa, and Nyukrumpa.[29]

The spiritual mentor Chengawa generally gave the following advice to his assembly of disciples: "In general, if you were to condense all the teachings—all three scriptural baskets and the two vehicles—they would be embodied in two: refraining from harming others and helping others. Forbearance is critical to put these two into practice, for without forbearance you will retaliate against the harm that others inflict upon you, and you do not turn away from causing harm when this happens. Without this forbearance there is no helping others. So to succeed in your Dharma practice, forbearance is essential.

"There are four methods of practicing forbearance: (1) practicing it in the fashion of putting up a target for shooting arrows, (2) practicing it by means of cultivating love and compassion, (3) practicing it in the fashion of a master and his pupil, and (4) practicing it by means of the nature of reality.

1. The first, *practicing forbearance in the fashion of putting up a target for shooting arrows*, is as follows. If you don't put up a target, it cannot be hit by an arrow; it is only because a target has been hoisted that the arrow can hit it. In the same manner, if you had not hoisted the target through your past karma, the arrows of harm would not have hit it in this life. So the arisal of harm perpetrated by others is due to your accumulation of negative karma in past lives. It is not appropriate, therefore, to become angry with others. The *Guide to the Bodhisattva's Way of Life* states:

> So if I do not wrong them,
> no one will wrong me in return.[30]

> Previously I, too, have caused such harm
> to other sentient beings;
> therefore this befalling of harm upon me—
> I who have harmed sentient beings—is just.[31]

Not only that, even in terms of this life, the effects of having inflicted harm on others when you were younger appear in later years. Likewise, the effects of last year's harm appear this year, last month's harm this month, and yesterday's harm today. Even in this very moment, if you hoist the target by speaking painful words to others and by negative behavior, right away the arrows of painful words and so on will fall upon you. Recognize therefore that it is because you put up the target that the arrows of harm from others have befallen you. With such awareness, refrain from anger toward others. This is what Chengawa taught.

2. *Practicing forbearance by means of love and compassion* is as follows. If a lunatic harms someone, others who are sane do not challenge the insane person; instead they say, 'Poor thing, what a pity!' and do not retaliate. In the same manner, reflect that those who harm you are deeply insane, possessed by demons with forceful afflictions. Thinking, 'How tragic!' cultivate compassion toward them. In a way, the lunatic who is possessed by a malevolent force is less insane, and the harm he inflicts is therefore of a lesser degree, for he harms only someone's body and life. As his insanity is confined to a few years, a few months, or a few days, it is shorter in duration. In contrast, when a human being with a 'sane' mind inflicts harm on other sentient beings, his insanity is graver. The duration of such insanity is longer, as he has been under the power of affliction since beginningless cyclic existence until now. And the impact of such harm is greater because his unrestrained indulgence in nonvirtue in body, speech, and mind gives rise to the sufferings of the three lower realms. Your compassion should therefore be even greater, so cultivate love and compassion toward those who harm you, and do not harbor anger toward them. The *Guide to the Bodhisattva's Way of Life* states:

> If, when they are under the sway of the afflictions,
> they kill even their own dear selves,
> how could it be that at such times [when afflicted]
> they would not injure others' bodies?

Under the sway of the afflictions, therefore,
some engage in acts such as killing themselves;
even if you feel no compassion,
how could you be angry at them?[32]

3. *Practicing forbearance in the fashion of a master and his pupil* is as follows. If there were no preceptor to confer the precepts, for instance, there would be no vows; if there were no master to give the teachings, there would be no knowledge [of the scriptures]. In the same manner, if you had no enemies to harm you, you would have no forbearance. Thus you should view those who assail you with verbal abuse and so on as teachers who grant you the gift of forbearance. Practicing sympathetic joy and repaying their kindness, view yourself as a student seeking to learn forbearance and do not be angry with them.

4. *Practicing forbearance in the form of the nature of reality* is as follows. On the ultimate level, all the factors—myself, the object of harm; the other, the agent of harm; and the act of harm itself—are emptiness, the ultimate nature of reality. All these perceptions, such as me being attacked, are apparitions of a deluded mind and are therefore like dreams and illusions. Seen this way it makes no sense to be angry with them. The *Guide to the Bodhisattva's Way of Life* states:

> Thus with respect to these empty things,
> what can be obtained, what can be lost?
> What can be disliked, what can be liked?
> Who can be humiliated as well?[33]

We do not remain angry toward a dream enemy after waking up from sleep and recognizing his lack of intrinsic existence. Likewise, our present enemies are, on the ultimate level, devoid of intrinsic existence, just like a dream. So instead of being hateful toward them, you should practice forbearance."

This is what Chengawa taught.

———∞∞∞———

Again, the spiritual mentor Chengawa said: "To attain liberation and omniscience you must train in a practice that is at variance with what worldly people do. For instance, the worldly cherish the buddhas more than sentient beings, they cherish themselves more than others, they cherish those who help them more than those who cause them harm, and they cherish pleasure more than hardship.

"Given that we must act in an inverse manner, we must cherish sentient beings more than the buddhas. Why? Because normally not even the slightest disrespect will arise toward the buddhas. There are in contrast four reasons we must cherish sentient beings: (1) we must cherish them on the grounds that all beings in cyclic existence are our parents; (2) since our parents are suffering in cyclic existence, we must cherish them by offering our help; (3) we must cherish sentient beings on the grounds that by helping them, our own welfare will be secured as a byproduct; and (4) we must cherish them on the grounds that by helping sentient beings we make offerings to all the buddhas and bodhisattvas and please them.

"Also, worldly people cherish themselves more than others. We on the other hand must cherish others more than ourselves. Why? Since beginningless time we ourselves have caused our own suffering; nobody else has made us suffer. We say at present that it is affliction that causes us to suffer; yet there is no such duality between afflictions and the self. So self is the enemy that has made us suffer in cyclic existence since beginningless time. It is necessary, therefore, to inflict as much damage as possible upon this enemy. As for others, we must cherish them. Why? Since it is in relation to other sentient beings that we accumulate merit, all the happiness in the world arises from them. Thus we must cherish them. Since it is on the basis of sentient beings that we can cultivate the two awakening minds, it is from them that all the higher qualities of nirvana come into being. Therefore we must cherish sentient beings.

"Worldly people cherish those who help them more than those who harm them. We, on the other hand, must do the opposite. Why? In worldly terms parents are the greatest source of benefit. Parents give their children estates, land, a house, gold, turquoise, horses, cattle, a wife, servants, and so on. From the point of view of Dharma practice, however, nothing is more harmful than this. For on the basis of having been given these objects of attachment, karma and affliction increase tremendously, leading thus to their further accumulation, which eventually becomes a factor for casting one into the hells. Although one's parents of this life may seem beneficial in the present, since they ultimately lead one to suffering, there is no greater enemy.[34] Therefore we must cherish those who cause us harm more than those who bring us benefit. Why? Due to an enemy's harm, we cultivate forbearance and thus obtain immeasurable merit. Because of our enemy's harm, we step up our efforts and traverse higher and higher spiritual levels, thereby achieving all higher attainments. So we must cherish those who harm us.

"Worldly people cherish pleasure more than hardship. We, on the other hand, must do the opposite, cherishing hardship more than pleasure. Why? Worldly people are attached to the pleasures of going to bed, sleeping, sex, laziness, clothes, and food, and these all cause suffering. We on the other hand must cherish hardship, because through the pains involved in serving teachers and members of the Sangha, performing ascetic practices of ethical discipline, and engaging in virtuous activities, our accumulations will be completed and obscurations purified. We will thereby attain the state of great bliss." Therefore, Chengawa said that we must cherish hardship. He said that since it is on the basis of physical illness and mental pain that we experience disenchantment with cyclic existence and generate true renunciation, we must cherish hardship.

Therefore, according to Chengawa, if you possess these four practices that are at variance with the worldly, then like the accurate divination of an oracle, you need not do anything at all. If you lack these four, then like a bad fortune-teller, nothing you do will be of any benefit.

———— ∞ ————

Again, the spiritual mentor Chengawa said: "At present, even the Dharma practices of the best practitioners are mixed with the concerns of this life.

First, fearing weakness, one holds on to the hems
    of a group.
Fearing abduction by ghosts, one does retreats on
    wrathful deities.
Fearing starvation in some future, one hoards possessions.
Fearing ill repute, one adopts all kinds of affected
    behavior.

"You may wish to attain buddhahood amid such pursuits, but it cannot happen. It is like wanting from the same sheep both a bag for carrying water and a sheepskin that can barely be lifted. It is not possible.

"How then should we act? If we practice forbearance instead of retaliation when someone harms us, a person with a harsh mouth cannot torment us. Since the best response to a harsh tongue is the practice of forbearance, we need not latch on to a group," Chengawa said.

"When enemies and obstacles seek opportunities to harm us, we recognize the self to be nonexistent on even the conventional level, like the horns of a rabbit. And since we have already given away our body to the ghosts, even the gods and demons of the billionfold universe cannot harm it. Since the best counterforce is the realization of no-self; we need not undertake mantra recitation of wrathful deities.

"Although we may have no possessions and provisions, we commit the core of our mind to Dharma practice, commit the core of our Dharma practice to the life of a beggar, and commit the end of this beggar's life to death. Therefore all those with faith will honor us. Since the best possession is a lack of attachment, we need not hoard material things.

"If others disparage us, since we have ensured that our minds are free of pretenses, we will become in the end an object of admiration for all. Since the best basis for fame and renown is flawless thought and behavior, we'll have no need at all to adopt pretentious behavior," said Chengawa.

Again, the spiritual mentor Chengawa said: "In general, it is on the basis of grasping at the self-existence of persons and the self-existence of phenomena that all affliction and distorted thought proliferates. In particular, for us it is the grasping at the self-existence of persons alone that causes harm. Therefore it is the self-existence of persons that is to be attacked and eliminated through the three levels of wisdom—the understandings derived from learning, from reflection, and from meditation. However, in our case, even while engaged in learning, reflection, and meditation, since our grasping at self increases, the strength of our forbearance is weaker than a deer calf, and our temperament remains more irritable than the ghost of Tsang.[35] These are signs that our understandings derived from learning, reflection, and meditation have gone wrong. If we view external appearances as somewhat empty, yet our inner self remains intact, without even a scratch, this is like shooting an arrow far away when the target is right in front of us. It is like searching for a thief's footprints in the meadow when he ran to the forest, or sending ritual *torma* cake to the northern gate while the ghost is at the eastern gate."

PHUCHUNGWA (1031–1106)

Phuchungwa, whose personal name was Shönu Gyaltsen, was one of the "three Kadam brothers." Like his brothers, Phuchungwa, too, met Master Atiśa and received teachings from him at Nyethang. Before his encounter with Atiśa, young Phuchungwa had studied with Khutön, especially the treatises related to the Perfection of Wisdom scriptures. He had also mastered the study of monastic discipline. Among the three famous brothers, it was Phuchungwa who first became a close disciple of Master Dromtönpa. The three brothers kept in close touch with each other, occasionally even exchanging specific teachings among themselves. Phuchungwa dedicated his life to single-pointed meditative practice and did not cultivate many students or found any monastery. Phuchungwa lived primarily as a hermit, first wandering in different places and living in caves, finally settling in the Phenpo region, where he built a small meditation place. It was at his hermitage that he taught individual meditators, focusing especially on meditations related to the principle of dependent origination. Among his students were such disciples as Shawo Gangpa and Ben Güngyal.

Phuchungwa is most revered as the founder of the "Kadam lineage of pith instructions" and as the inheritor of Atiśa and Dromtönpa's teachings enshrined in the *Book of Kadam*. He is also credited with being the source of the mind-training practice known as the "heart of dependent origination," a text of which can be found in *Mind Training: The Great Collection*.[36]

The spiritual mentor Phuchungwa said: "We have obtained this utterly fragile human existence of leisure and opportunity. Although we have obtained it, we don't have the power to stay long, for we must all die. At the time of death we have no power to retain all the mundane thoughts regarding this life and the mundane beauties, not even the fallen petal of a flower. Nothing can accompany us. At that time everything will be revealed starkly: the level of our intelligence, the strength or weakness of our ability, and our skillfulness or its lack in the pursuit of our goals.

"If at the time of death we remain joyful and rest in a warm glow, then our level of intelligence is high, our ability is strong, and our pursuit of goals is skillful. Such a person is called competent. But if at that time vivid visions appear of Yama's form and aspects of the lower realms, we have not been skilled in the pursuit of goals and have thus failed to be competent. Most of us travel mistaken paths because of continually reinforcing the habit of planning for this life.

"It is inconceivable that the fully awakened perfect Buddha would utter falsehoods. It is also impossible that the great authors of treatises, such as Master Nāgārjuna, would speak falsely. It is also impossible that the sublime teachers would speak falsely. So the question is, 'Who then puts us on the false paths?' It is our desires pertaining to this life that have led us to the false paths, so we should constantly contemplate death and, by recalling death, ensure we never remain attached to our selfish interests. We should meditate on the defects of cyclic existence in its entirety and, by bringing disenchantment to mind, ensure we never become attached to any part of cyclic existence. We should meditate on emptiness—the ultimate mode of being of all things—and, by recalling no-self, ensure we never become attached to things and their signs."

Again, the spiritual mentor Phuchungwa said: "If you are practicing Dharma seriously, you should be like a writing board with holes in it. Just as a writing board with holes cannot be used for inscribing taxes, you should be someone who cannot remain together with those who are concerned only with this life.[37] Excessive befriending and appeasing of others will lead you to be abducted by the māras, so not appeasing others is something to be desired. Because he is not pleased, he does not come; and because he disparages you, others do not come either. In such situations, though you may have only a single *shogang* coin[38] for your provisions, while it lasts your mental state will remain joyful and you will be able to engage in virtuous activities. When virtuous activities increase, higher qualities come about naturally. Then even the welfare of others will come about spontaneously."

Again, the spiritual mentor Phuchungwa said:

> Greater is the bliss of eliminating sensual desires than the bliss of indulging them.
>
> Greater is it to know a single meaning than to know many words.
>
> Greater are the benefits of giving teachings than the benefits of giving many material things.
>
> Greater is the fear of the suffering of future lives than the fear of this life's suffering.
>
> Greater is it to resolve doubts within one's mind than doubts about outer meanings of words.

NYUKRUMPA (1042–1109)

Nyukrumpa, whose personal name was Tsöndrü Bar, was principally a student of Chengawa, youngest of the three Kadam brothers. He founded two Kadam monasteries in central Tibet, Nyukrum (from which the nickname Nyukrumpa is derived) and Thangkya. Following construction of the first monastery, his master Chengawa visited the newly built monastery and consecrated the site as a representation of the holy Buddhist site of Bodhgaya. Only scant biographical information on Nyukrumpa is available. From a wider historical perspective, Nyukrumpa's importance lies in having been one of the Kadam teachers from whom Gampopa, a principal founder of the Kagyü school, received instructions.

Spiritual mentor Nyukrumpa said:

Those who wish for birth in higher realms and achieve the definite goodness of enlightenment should cultivate recognition of cyclic existence as a prison.

They should cultivate recognition of their body and life as bubbles in water.

They should cultivate recognition of evil friends as an enemy's henchmen.

They should cultivate recognition of their teachers as wish-granting jewels.

They should cultivate recognition of afflictions as venomous snakes.

They should cultivate recognition of negative karma as deadly poison.

They should cultivate recognition of sensual objects as fire buried in ashes.

They should cultivate recognition of fame and renown as echoes.

They should cultivate recognition of gifts and honor as snares or nets.

They should cultivate recognition of evil friends as a plague.

They should cultivate recognition of positive friends as a fortress.

They should cultivate recognition of all sentient beings as fathers and mothers.

They should cultivate recognition of giving as a wish-granting cow.[39]

They should cultivate recognition of morality as a precious ornament.

They should cultivate recognition of forbearance as an excellent armor.

They should cultivate recognition of joyous effort as a heavenly horse.

They should cultivate recognition of concentration as a great treasure.

They should cultivate recognition of wisdom derived through learning, reflection, and meditation as a lamp.

KHAMLUNGPA (1025–1115)

Khamlungpa Shākya Yönten was a principal student of Dromtönpa, sometimes identified as a fourth Kadam brother. Khamlungpa met with Master Atiśa at a young age. It was, however, Dromtönpa whom he would seek to be his main teacher. As his name suggests, Khamlungpa founded the monastery of Khamlung, where, over time, around eight hundred monks converged. He was particularly famed for his altruistic temperament. It is said that everyone who saw him developed deep admiration.

Khamlungpa is identified as the source of the instructions on "mind training in eight sessions," whereby the practitioner learns to relate all key aspects of everyday life to the mind-training practice of cultivating and enhancing the awakening mind. A concise instruction on this special mind training can be found in *Mind Training: The Great Collection.*[40]

Spiritual mentor Khamlungpa said:

> Since it is extremely hard to obtain a human existence of leisure and opportunity, guard morality as you would protect your own eyes.
> Since there is no knowing when this illusory aggregation might come to an end, strive in spiritual activities through body and speech.
> Since all conditioned positive karmas are [ultimately insignificant and] neutral, make extensive aspirations for the benefit of sentient beings.
> Since everything is transient and illusory, grasp at no thing as substantially real and let go of clinging.

BEN GÜNGYAL (ELEVENTH CENTURY)

Ben Güngyal, known also as Ben Jakpa (*jakpa* means "robber" in Tibetan), was the famous bandit-turned-meditator. His personal name was Tsültrim Gyalwa. Suffering from poverty as a young man, Ben Güngyal is said to have adopted the life of a robber prior to becoming a revered yogi. He was a principal student of the Kadam master Gönpawa (1016–82), as well as of all three Kadam brothers. Ben would often use his previous identity as a robber and his monastic identity as the monk Tsültrim Gyalwa as a means of cultivating and maintaining constant self-awareness. Whenever he perceived lapses in his thought, he would chastise himself, "Now I am the monk Tsültrim Gyalwa. You, Ben Güngyal, stop being a demon-like nuisance to the monk Tsültrim Gyalwa!"

There are some memorable stories about Ben Güngyal's ruthless honesty and critical self-awareness. When a patron invited Ben Güngyal to his home, at one point Ben Güngyal's hand habitually reached out to steal something. Catching himself he grabbed his right arm with his left and shouted, "Thief, thief!" When the hosts appeared and asked where the thief was, he showed his right arm and said, "Here he is." On another occasion Ben Güngyal received news that his patron wished to come and visit his meditation cave. Ben Güngyal became excited and started tidying up, including filling the water bowls on the altar with fresh water. After having cleaned up his place, he sat down to rest. Just then he realized what he had done: he had fallen victim to the mundane concern of seeking approval. So he went outside and picked up a handful of earth and threw it into the air so that his place would look untidy as usual![41]

⸰⸰⸰

Spiritual mentor Ben Jakpa proclaimed the following as a counsel to his own heart:

73

Since you lack power even over today's lifespan, do not plan
for a permanent stay, O monk.

Cling not to this illusory collection as a self, O monk.

Grasp not as dual that which is by nature nondual, O monk.

Cultivate love and compassion for those who have failed to
realize this, O monk.

Since you must plant the seeds of your ultimate goal in
this very life, summon courage and joyful perseverance,
O monk.

KHARAK GOMCHUNG (CA. ELEVENTH CENTURY)

Known also by the shorter name Kharakpa, this Kadam master's personal name was Wangchuk Lodrö. Born in Tsang province in central Tibet, Kharakpa was one of the principal disciples of the Kadam teacher Gönpawa. Initially, Kharakpa began as a student of the Dzokchen master Aro Jangchup Yeshé, but after the death of this teacher, Kharakpa spent seven years at Radreng at the feet of Naljorpa and Gönpawa, where he received all the major spiritual instructions stemming from Master Atiśa. Later he lived as a hermit meditating in caves. It was during his period as a hermit that Kharakpa developed a close collegial relationship with the Kadam teacher Potowa, the two of them often sharing with each other personal experiences and insights derived from their practices. Because of his Dzokchen background, Kharakpa's teachings are considered a fusion of Dzokchen and Kadam, somewhat analogous to Gampopa's fusion of Kadam and Mahamudra on the Kagyü side.

Kharakpa came to be revered as a perfect example of a true renunciate, single-pointedly dedicated to meditative practice and compassionate action. He is perhaps most known for his highly practical and concise teachings, most of which pertain to the central issue of overcoming attachment to the mundane concerns of this life. These teachings later became known collectively as the "three cycles of Kharakpa": (1) the Twelve Points of the Stages of the Path, (2) the Seventy Pieces of Advice, and (3) the Training in the Awakening Mind. Although the complete texts of Kharak Gomchung's first and the last cycles appear to be no longer extant, large sections of the author's work on the first cycle can be found in Chenga Lodrö Gyaltsen's *Initial Mind Training: Opening the Door of Dharma*. The entire text of the second cycle, the Seventy Pieces of Advice, is found in Yeshé Döndrup's *Treasury of Gems*.[42]

Once when spiritual mentor Kharak Gomchung was visiting Chenga Monastery, Yeshé Sung, the teacher from Gyal, said, "I would like to request from you, O spiritual mentor, a method for engaging in spiritual activities."

The spiritual mentor Kharakpa replied, "There are three levels to the method of engaging in spiritual activities. The lowest level of spiritual activity is to avoid harming sentient beings; the middle level of spiritual activity is to help sentient beings; and the highest level of spiritual activity, since both self and sentient beings cannot be objectified, is to meditate on the unborn nature."

—— ⚬⚬⚬ ——

Again, the spiritual mentor Kharakpa said:

> Since no aspect of higher qualities grows in a person who lacks faith, seek a spiritual mentor and read the sutras.
> Since no aspect of higher qualities grows in a person who lacks joyful perseverance, contemplate death and impermanence and shun laziness.
> Since no aspect of higher qualities grows in a person who is vain, lower your head and adopt humility.

"If you possess these three practices, you will be a suitable basis for the śrāvaka's path, a suitable basis for the bodhisattva path, and a suitable basis for the path of secret mantra as well. In brief, you will be a suitable basis for all higher qualities."

—— ⚬⚬⚬ ——

Again, the spiritual mentor Kharakpa said:

> Since attachment prevents you from transcending cyclic existence, you err if you do not view it as a flaw.

Since aversion destroys virtues from their root, you err if
you do not view it as a flaw.

Since vanity prevents growth of extraordinary higher qualities and weakens the roots of virtue, you err if you do not
view it as a flaw.

Since generosity brings forth the perfect resources of gods
and humans, you err if you deride giving.

Since morality brings forth the extraordinary existence of
the higher realms, you err if you deride morality.

Since compassion is the root of all Great Vehicle teachings,
you err if you deride compassion.

Since the bodhisattva vows are an extraordinary method for
cultivating omniscience, you err if you deride the bodhisattva vows.

Since swift accomplishment of common and uncommon
higher attainments depends upon secret mantra, you err
if you deride the commitments of secret mantra.

<hr />

Again, the spiritual mentor Kharakpa said:

The ultimate view is to be free of all positions.

The ultimate meditation is to be free of all mental
engagements.

The ultimate action is to be free of all affirmations and
rejections.

The ultimate practice is to be free of all experiences.

DRAKGYAPA (ELEVENTH CENTURY)

This was probably the senior student of Dromtönpa known as Jolek, a monk from Drakgyap Monastery. Jolek is said to have originally met Atiśa when the Indian master was in western Tibet. Later, traveling as an attendant to Dromtönpa, he became one of the closest students of Master Dromtönpa, alongside the three Kadam brothers, and completely dedicated himself to studying at Drom's feet. He is said to have received a wide range of teachings from Dromtönpa, covering both sutra and tantra, including the more esoteric instructions as well.[43]

⸻

The spiritual mentor Drakgyapa said: "If we wish from our heart to act in accord with Dharma, we should regularly meditate on death and impermanence and turn our backs on the mundane aspirations of this life. For even if we were to achieve all three—joy, happiness, and fame—in this life, if our thoughts are not turned toward Dharma, these will all be tricksters. Swiftly we must shun them so that we have no connection with them. They are to be discarded one day anyway, so if we let go of them today, it will be worthwhile.

"Even if we are renowned as learned ones, disciplined ones, teachers, and meditators, if we fail to give up [attachment to] this life, we will pursue only the means for achieving greatness in this life. In this way, we will need to cover the entire earth with our restless pursuits, and through this we will become forcibly and strongly saturated with negative karma, increasingly at odds with the Dharma. Continuing to think 'I will not die,' we will die with clinging and attachment, with the chores of this life left unfinished. For us there is nowhere to go but to the lower realms. If, on the other hand, the realization of death and imper-manence has arisen in our minds and we have forsaken [attach-

78

ment to] this life, we may not have been renowned in our lives as learned ones or as disciplined ones, but we will accomplish all aims without others knowing of it. Because of having made exclusive preparations for death, we will be able to die happily and joyfully, free of any attachment or clinging to anything, no matter when we die.

"Therefore our approach should be like this. Keeping death and impermanence in your hearts, examine whether all the things we have done in the past, all that we are doing now, and all that we intend to do in the future are mixed with [the mundane aims of] this life. If they turn out to be mixed with [the mundane aims of] this life, they have become mixed with affliction, so relinquish all the afflictions and negative karma falsely construed as Dharma practices. To relinquish these, persistently and repeatedly apply the vigilance of mindfulness, the observation of introspective awareness, and the restraint of heedfulness. You may have made many efforts driven by [attachment to] this life, but on the morrow of death you will have to depart naked and empty-handed, so take death for your pillow instead, and engage in a Dharma practice untainted by thoughts of this life.

Given that between tomorrow and the next life no one knows which will come first, to implement this ideal, starting now and before tomorrow arrives, offer all your material possessions toward the accumulation of merit, declare and purify whatever remorse you harbor in your heart, train your mind toward all the objects of mind training, strive to the best of your ability in whatever Dharma practices you know, make all imaginable aspiration prayers for the benefit of the sentient beings, and so on. Act as though you have no choice but to do these things.

Given that between next month and the next life no one knows which will come first, starting now and before next month arrives, act as though you have no choice but to do this.

Given that between tomorrow morning and the next life no one knows which will come first, starting now and before tomorrow morning arrives, act as though you have no choice but to do this.

Given that you have no control over even this evening's lifespan, this very day, offer your material possessions toward the accumulation of merit, declare and purify any remorse in your heart, make extensive aspiration prayers, engage in meditative absorptions, and so on. Act as though you have no choice but to do these.

"From the very morning of our birth, the only definite thing ahead is death. There is also no certainty as to when this death will strike, so we must consistently behave as if our death were likely to come this very evening."

Neusurpa (1042–1118)

Neusurpa Yeshé Bar was born the very year the Indian master Atiśa arrived in western Tibet. At a young age he joined the monastery of Drakgyap, where he is said to have served in the administration of the monastery for a year. Even as a young monk Neusurpa became famed for his natural capacity for stable meditative concentration. A senior lama from the Drakgyap region who happened to be in central Tibet went to see the Kadam master Gönpawa and spoke to him of this precocious young monk. Upon his return this elder monk urged young Neusurpa to go to Radreng Monastery to study and practice at the feet of Master Gönpawa. Thus began his long relationship with the master. After Gönpawa's death Neusurpa became a disciple of all three Kadam brothers, especially Master Potowa.

Neusurpa is especially known as the inheritor of Gönpawa's teachings on the stages of the path (*lamrim*) instructions. Notes compiled by Neusurpa's students on his stages of the path instructions came to be widely disseminated in Tibet. He founded the monastery of Neusur (from which he came to derive his title Neusurpa), where around two thousand monks converged. His students included such luminaries as Gyergompa, Gezé Jangchup, Thakmapa, and the adept Nyiphukpa.[44]

Spiritual mentor Neusurpa said:

> Since one cannot attain buddhahood with conceptualization of enemies and friends, recognize all sentient beings equally as your mother.

> Since one cannot attain buddhahood with conceptualization of ordinariness, recognize all sentient beings equally as meditation deities.

Since one cannot attain buddhahood with conceptualization of signs, recognize all phenomena as equal in their emptiness, the ultimate nature of reality.

LANGRI THANGPA (1054–1123)

Langri Thangpa was a prominent student of the Kadam master Potowa. Born the year Master Atiśa passed away, Langri Thangpa became a monk and acquired the monastic name Dorjé Sengé. From a young age he came to be revered as an emanation of Buddha Amitābha as well as the reincarnation of the famed Tibetan translator Kawa Peltsek. Never settling permanently in one spot, Langri Thangpa moved from place to place, studying at the feet of all three Kadam brothers, most of all upholding the teachings and instructions of Master Potowa. When Master Potowa was dying, he is said to have given the following advice to Langri Thangpa: "Do not tie yourself to any one place. Do not hold even a single thing as your own. Keep these two points in your heart."

Langri Thangpa is particularly famed for his great compassion. Because of constantly contemplating the sufferings of all sentient beings, Langri Thangpa was often in tears and came to be known as "Langthangpa with the weeping downcast face." Distilling the essence of the teachings of mind training, Langri Thangpa composed the celebrated *Eight Verses on Mind Training*, which contains expressions of such powerful sentiments as "May I take upon myself the defeat and offer to others the victory," and "May I cherish those of unpleasant character as a precious treasure rarely found," and so on. Langri Thangpa founded Langthang Monastery in Phenpo in 1093, which attracted around two thousand monks during his lifetime. His principal student was Shawo Gangpa, and the early Kagyü lineage master Phakmo Drupa also received teachings from him. Langri Thangpa's *Eight Verses on Mind Training* as well as a succinct commentary to this text can be found in the companion volume *Essential Mind Training*.[45]

Spiritual mentor Langri Thangpa said:

> Since one person cannot fathom the measure of another, do not belittle anyone.
>
> Since all teachings of the Buddha bring results, do not engage in them with discriminations of "good ones" and "bad ones."
>
> Since the welfare of sentient beings is a Mahayana practitioner's only task, ensure that your armor of working for the welfare of others is not weak.
>
> Since you cannot lead others without attaining a secure ground for yourself, strive hard in your meditation practices in solitude.

SHARAWA (1070–1141)

Sharawa Yönten Drak was a principal student of Potowa. He and Langri Thangpa were together known as the "sun and moon-like disciples of Master Potowa." From a young age, Sharawa came to be recognized for his great intelligence, prompting some to recognize him as an emanation of Mañjuśrī, the buddha of wisdom. Although he received teachings from all three Kadam brothers, Sharawa primarily stayed at the feet of Potowa, eventually becoming the main custodian of Potowa's lineage. Sharawa founded the monastery of Shara (from which he acquired his title) in the Tré region of Phenpo, which is said to have attracted around three thousand monks during his lifetime.

A key spiritual heritage descended from Sharawa is the codification of the scattered instructions of Master Atiśa pertaining to mind-training practice. Although subsequent Tibetan writers attribute the authorship of the *Seven-Point Mind Training* to Chekawa, it was in fact Master Sharawa who first formulated the mind-training teachings into the framework of the seven points. His student Chekawa happened to be the one who first inscribed it into a text. Sharawa's students included Chekawa, Tapkapa, Tumtön Lodrö Drak (founder of Narthang Monastery), and Naljorpa Sherap Dorjé.[46]

Spiritual mentor Sharawa said:

> Since [attachment to] women is a root of affliction, do not
>   seek them where you are.[47]
> Since alcohol is a root of affliction, do not drink it even
>   under threat of death.
> Since travel is a root of affliction, do not engage in excessive
>   travel.
> Since hoarding things is a root of affliction, relinquish
>   grasping and attachment.

85

JAYÜLWA (1075–1138)

Jayülwa Shönu Ö was the principal disciple of Master Chengawa, one of the three Kadam brothers. As a young novice Jayülwa became a close student of Chengawa, often serving him as a personal attendant as well. Once a senior student of the master, Tölungpa, came to see his teacher. So impressed by the young novice, he is said to have remarked, "With respect to devotion, this young novice excels me. His intelligence is greater than mine, his diligence is superior to mine, and his compassion is greater than mine." When Master Chengawa was dying he advised Jayülwa thus: "Do not let yourself fall victim to worldly conventions, and do not take full monastic ordination." Years later when circumstances called for Jayülwa to take full monastic ordination, he is said to have sought a way to receive his late master's permission to do so.

Jayülwa was known for his single-pointed meditative practice of the key themes of the Kadam teachings—contemplation of death and impermanence, deep conviction in the law of karma, true renunciation of mundane concerns and ambitions, cultivation of the altruistic wish for awakening based on compassion for all beings, cultivation of the wisdom realizing the emptiness of all things. He is also known for a series of mystical experiences, including visionary encounters with Indian masters such as Nāgabodhi. Jayülwa founded the monastery of Jayül (from which he came to acquire his nickname), and his students included Gyergompa, Tromsherwa, Tsangpa Rinpoché, Drakmarwa, and Gampopa, a founding father of the Kagyü school who subsequently became a principal student of the much-revered poet-saint Milarepa.[48]

Spiritual mentor Jayülwa said:

> Since it is the foundation and the basis of the path to libera-
> tion and omniscience, observe pure morality.
> Since it is the axle of the path to liberation and omni-
> science, train in the awakening mind.
> Since it is the staircase of the path to liberation and
> omniscience, strive constantly to gather the two
> accumulations.
> Since he is the navigator on the path to liberation and
> omniscience, always rely on the spiritual mentor.

⸺⧢⸺

Again, the spiritual mentor Jayülwa said:

> Subject and object are like sandalwood and its scent.
> Samsara and nirvana are like water and ice.
> Appearance and emptiness are clouds and the sky.
> Conceptualizations and the nature of reality are like waves
> and the ocean.

TÖLUNGPA (1032–1116)

Tölungpa Rinchen Nyingpo was an important student of Master Chengawa and of the yogi Naljorpa Amé. At a young age Tölungpa went to Tsang province in central Tibet and extensively studied both sutra and tantra. A talented debater, he participated in a major scholarly discussion that took place over a series of days in central Tibet attended by a large number of the top scholars of the day. Tölungpa overheard a remark by an observer, one Logkya Tsogen, that the participants were obsessed with the "white-spotted cow" (a reference to a debate in the philosophy of language), a discussion that ran on at length until one's skull cracked open, and that not even four words in the discussion were on how to overcome samsara and attain liberation. Agreeing with these sentiments, Tölungpa developed a desire to go to India to seek the Dharma. Just then he heard someone say the following lines:

> Life is short and the fields of knowledge numerous,
> and no one knows how long one's life will be.
> So just as a swan extracts the milk mixed with water,
> pursue only those subjects you truly aspire for.

Upon enquiring whose lines those were, Tölungpa learned that they were advice given by the Indian master Atiśa. This led Tölungpa to go to Radreng Monastery, where he became a close disciple of Naljorpa, who had by then succeeded Dromtönpa as head of the monstery. After Naljorpa's death, Tölungpa took Master Chengawa as his principal spiritual teacher. His students included Tokden Dingpopa, Geshé Lhaso, and Ja Dülzin.[49]

The spiritual mentor Tölungpa said:

If you aspire for liberation from your heart, follow after
    the disciplined rather than the learned;
follow after the practitioner rather than the preacher;
follow after the humble rather than the high;
follow after the friend with faith rather than the friend
    with intelligence.

"We are not pitiful because we lack knowledge of the teachings; we are so because of befriending people who do not act in accord with the Dharma."

— ∞ —

Again, the spiritual mentor Tölungpa said:

Grasp not at appearances that are constructs as
    substantially real.
Place not your hope in conditioned phenomena.
Grieve not over the dismantling of illusions.
Weaken not the antidotes against desire and the afflictions.
Embrace not the eight mundane concerns.
Prolong not your association with negative friends.
Harbor not excessive love and affection in your relations
    with loved ones.
Weaken not your faith and respect for your teachers
    and the Three Jewels.
Be not attached to your body and possessions.
Weaken not your dedication to learning, reflection,
    and meditation.
Shower not with special praise the distractions of gifts
    and honor.
Weaken not your resilience when facing hardships in
    Dharma practice.
Weaken not your altruistic compassion free of clinging.

Nambarwa (twelfth century)

Nambarwa was one of the "eight great students" of Jayülwa Shönu Ö (1075–1138), as well as one of the "four senior sons" of the spiritual mentor Laksorwa, who was, in turn, a student of the translator Naktso Lotsāwa (1011–64). Nambarwa is known mostly for having penned extensive notes on the stages of the path (*lamrim*) instructions stemming from Naktso based on teachings he had received from his own teacher Laksorwa. These notes are unfortunately no longer extant. Nambarwa founded the monasteries of Nambar and Rampa Lhading and held the abbotship of Sangphu Monastery for eight years. Beyond this scant information there is very little available on the life of this Kadam master.[50]

Spiritual mentor Nambarwa said:

If you fail to feel disenchanted with the cycle of existence in the three realms, your mind will not engage with liberation, so meditate on the defects of samsara in its entirety.

If you do not decisively end attachment and clinging, your bondage to sensual objects will not be cut, so forsake material possessions as if they were gobs of spit.

If you do not possess the substantial causes, the blessings of spiritual mentors will not enter you, so cultivate the recognition of your teachers as buddhas.

If you do not regularly meditate on impermanence, you will be confined to this mundane life, so mentally cultivate awareness of the scarcity of time.

If you fail to train the mind within, you will not be sustained by altruistic resolve at all times, so train in the awakening mind.

CHIMPHUPA (TWELFTH CENTURY)

There is very little available on the life of this Kadam master other than the fact that he was one of the "four senior sons" of Laksorwa, a key student of the translator Naktso Lotsāwa (1011–64). Each of these four sons of Laksorwa is said to have compiled notes from Laksorwa's teachings, focusing especially on the stages of the path (*lamrim*) instructions stemming from Naktso. Ja Dülzin compiled a condensed collection of notes that contain both stories and instructions; Chimphupa's notes contain few stories but extensive instructions; Nambarwa's notes contain only instructions with no stories; and Shulenpa's notes contain extensive stories and extensive instructions.

Once a tantric practitioner requested instruction from the spiritual mentor Chimphupa. The master responded:

> This world of appearance is an illusion; grasp it not as substantially real.
> The body is flesh and blood; grasp it not excessively as self.
> Material goods are fruits of past karma; exert not too much effort.
> Whatever you do is suffering; have not too many chores.
> The cycle of existence is suffering; embrace it not.

"As for other essential instructions, I will give them to you later when there is a long day."

SHAWO GANGPA (1067–1131)

Known also as Shawopa Pema Jangchup, this master was an important student of both Potowa and Phuchungwa, two of the three Kadam
brothers. Over time he became a key disciple of Langri Thangpa, the
author of *Eight Verses on Mind Training*, on the basis of whose teachings Shawopa gained profound realization of the awakening mind. He
founded the monastery of Shawogang, where thousands of monks
congregated and from which he came to acquire the name Shawopa
or Shawo Gangpa. There is very little biographical information on this
master despite the fact that his numerous spiritual sayings came to
enjoy wide appreciation and affection, as illustrated by the number of
sayings included in the present collection.[51]

⸻

The spiritual mentor Shawo Gangpa said: "Today, at this junc-
ture when we have obtained a human existence of leisure and
opportunity, met with a spiritual mentor, and encountered
the Mahayana teachings, we should strive our best to prepare
the bed for our future lives and plant the feet of liberation and
omniscience.

"First, to prepare the bed for our future lives, we must
strive our best to eradicate the ten negative karmas from their
roots and embrace the ten virtues. For this, we need to forsake
[attachment to] this life. To attain liberation we must avert our
thoughts from every part of cyclic existence. To plant the feet of
omniscience, we must train in the awakening mind within our
mental continuums.

"To generate these three thoughts we must accumulate merit,
for without gathering merit we will not be able to understand
the teachings. Even if we do understand the teachings in some
instances, their realization will not grow in us. Even if some

fragmented realizations grow in us, they will evaporate and will be of no benefit. Therefore the reason we wandered in cyclic existence in the past was from failing to accumulate merit and from collecting demerit. Even in this life our failure to have things as we wish is due to our failure to accumulate merit and eradicate negative, nonvirtuous karmas from their roots. Thus the foundation of all teachings can be subsumed into two—accumulating merit and purifying negative karma."

—∞∞∞—

Again, Shawopa said: "As for us, the desires of this life are what bring the suffering of this and future lives, so we should shun the things craved by attachment to this mundane life. When the objectives of this life's desire are extensive, our mind lacks peace; we wander everywhere, and in the course of this, all three factors—negative karma, suffering, and ill repute—strike simultaneously. We must therefore relinquish this multipronged mind of desire. When we succeed in turning away the mind of desire, that is when joy and happiness starts.

> We seek happiness in this life and throughout all our
>   lives, and so, as a sign of this, hoard nothing and crave
>   nothing in your heart.
> When you do not crave gifts, it is the best gift.
> When you do not crave praise, it is the best praise.
> When you do not crave fame, it is the best fame.
> When you do not crave followers, it is the best follower.

"If you wish to practice the Dharma from your heart, turn the tip of your mind toward the life of a beggar. Ensure that this life of a beggar ends with death.[52]

"If you are able to nurture this kind of attitude, you will certainly be free from distress caused by any of the three—gods, ghosts, and humans. If, on the other hand, you seek to slake the thirst[53] of the desires of this life, things like the following will happen: you will disgrace yourself; you will create your own miseries; others will ridicule you, while you yourself will be miserable; and in the future you will depart to the lower realms.

"Therefore, if you abandon broadcasting [your good deeds], adopt humility, relinquish desire, forsake all non-Dharma activities, and strive well in the meditative practices, the following things will happen: you will be happy, others will admire you, and in the future you will attain enlightenment. In brief, on our part we may initiate all kinds of endeavors, know all sorts of things, and engage in all kinds of deeds, but as long as our thoughts are not turned away from the desires of this life, no matter how much we say, we have no means of gaining the happiness of both this and future lives. If our thoughts are turned against all forms of desire, we need no longer search for happiness."

⸻ ∽◦◦◦∾ ⸻

Again, the spiritual mentor Shawopa said:

> Be not like those who, while failing to control themselves, seek to control others.
>
> Be not like those who, while lacking higher qualities within their mindstreams, aspire to be others' masters.
>
> Be not like those who, despite possessing great faith, fail to refrain from negative acts.
>
> Be not like those who, while admiring emptiness, possess excessive self-grasping.
>
> Be not like those who, despite having great intelligence, fail to recognize what is Dharma and what is not Dharma.
>
> Be not like those who, despite having sharp intelligence, fail to understand the teachings.

Be not like those who, while refraining from slight negative
  deeds, fail to shy away from grave ones.
Be not like those who, while having great altruistic motives,
  fail to avoid harming others.
Be not like those who, while they cannot live alone, are
  incapable of being in the company of others.
Be not like those who, while desiring to be disciplined, have
  little endurance.
Be not like those who, while being very generous in the
  short term, have little flexibility deep down.
Be not like those who, while their teachings are high, have
  low realization.
Be not like those who, while their masters are excellent,
  have bad behavior.
Be not like those who, while delighting in study of the
  teachings, dislike implementing them.
Be not like those who, while desiring solitude, delight in
  socializing with others.
Be not like those who, while desiring excellence, remain
  beset with extreme greed.
Be not like those who, while aspiring for liberation, let
  whatever they do slide into the eight mundane concerns.

———— ∞ ————

Again, the spiritual mentor Shawopa chastised himself:

You confounded one—you yearn for the high teachings for
  your inferior mentality!
You old mind—you hope improvement will occur while
  you do not improve yourself!
You heartless one—you act as if Dharma were important
  for others and base behavior for yourself!

You distorted one—you preach appropriate acts to others
and engage in inappropriate conduct yourself!

You who are like a pile of earth with steep slopes—
you have more backsliding than progression!

You expert in fickleness—you are elaborate in your
promises but brief in implementation!

You of wrong livelihood—you seek the afflictions and
pretend to apply their remedies!

You who are wrought with hopes and fears—you hope
that others will see your qualities and fear that others
will see your faults!

You seek victory over Dharma colleagues while accepting
loss from relatives!

You seek victory over the antidotes while accepting defeat
at the hands of the afflictions!

You seek victory in this life while accepting loss in future
lives!

You seek victory for those who perpetrate harm while
accepting loss for those who bring benefits!

You fail to understand that causing harm to others also
harms yourself!

You fail to understand that helping others also helps
yourself!

You fail to understand that harm and suffering are
conditions favorable to Dharma practice!

You fail to understand that desire and happiness are
obstacles to Dharma practice!

You proclaim the importance of Dharma practice to
others and then do not act in accord with Dharma
yourself!

You despise others for committing negative acts and
then fail to curtail your own ongoing negative deeds!

You fail to detect your own grave shortcomings and
then highlight even the slightest faults of others!

You curtail your altruistic deeds when no reward is
   forthcoming!

You cannot bear to see other practitioners being offered
   gifts and honor!

You love the high and are hostile toward the weak!

You dislike stories about the next life!

You lose your temper when others correct your flaws!

You hope others detect your virtues but do not allow
   others to become aware of your negative karma!

You are content when your external behavior is good even
   when your inner thoughts remain base!

You regard the pursuit of material things and objects of
   desire as joy and happiness!

You fail to search for happiness within and search for it
   instead outside!

You pledged to follow in the footsteps of the Buddha
   but follow instead after those of the worldly!

You consult the bodhisattvas but treasure items for sale
   in the hells!

You dedicate your body, resources, and virtues of the
   three times to sentient beings, and then fail to let go
   "I" and "self"!

You fail to understand that the affection of negative
   friends is the prelude to doom!

You fail to understand that the anger of virtuous friends
   is a source of benefit.

Because you'll waste so much time on "what is" and
   "what is not," do not indulge in chatter with others.

Because it will lead to the proliferation of craving, do not
   reign over a kingdom in your mind.

Because there is greater risk than profit, do not delight in
   making promises.

Because it will surely undermine your virtuous activities,
   give up excessive activities.

Relating these chastisements to his heart, Shawopa offered such counsel.

———— ✖ ————

Here, I, the monk Chegom, have collected and compiled together the scattered sayings of the Kadam masters, which constitute the heart advice of the sublime masters of Master Atiśa's lineage.

4. The Numerical Sayings of Kharak Gomchung

This supplement, consisting of selected sayings of Master Kharak Gom-chung, or Kharakpa, organized around numerical sets, was compiled by Geshé Lhopa, a student of the master himself.[54] The brief biographi-cal sketch of Kharakpa provided earlier mentioned his fusion of Dzok-chen and Kadam teachings. By the time Geshé Lhopa met his master Kharakpa, the former was already an established figure with special knowledge of the Maitreya cycle of classical Indian Buddhist texts, which includes *Ornament of Mahayana Scriptures* and the *Sublime Continuum*. After hearing of Kharakpa's fame, Lhopa went to see the master and requested teaching. Lhopa received extensive teachings from Master Kharakpa over a period of eight years.

Geshé Lhopa is reputed to have experienced a vision of the buddha of compassion, Avalokiteśvara, in his thousand-armed form. He was famed for being meticulous in his observance of all the vows and pre-cepts he had taken. It is said that at the point of death this master per-formed a full confession and purification rite pertaining to his monastic vows and undertook the self-empowerment rite as a form of tantric purification. Yeshé Döndrup, the nineteenth-century author of *Trea-sury of Gems*, speculates that the custom at Tashi Khyil Monastery in Amdo for dying monks to engage in empowerment rites was probably inspired by Geshé Lhopa's example.[55]

Homage to the sublime teachers!

I present here the sayings by summarizing into six sets of three, six sets of four, eight sets of five, five sets of six, and a set of seven.

Six sets of three
The first set of three, the three necessities, is:
1. Initially, it's necessary to fear death.
2. In the middle, it's necessary to have no remorse if death were to come.
3. Finally, it is necessary to face death without fear.

Three things are to be abandoned:
1. Abandon your place of birth.
2. Abandon home and family.
3. Abandon activities and chores.

Three things are to be embraced:
1. If you embrace a teacher, essential instructions will flow.
2. If you embrace meditation, experience will grow.
3. If you embrace meditative absorptions, realizations will increase.

Avoid the three [common] confusions:
1. A Dharma practitioner and pretender are liable to be confused.
2. The view and words are liable to be confused.
3. Meditation and intention are liable to be confused.

There are three methods of meditation:
1. Initially, meditate on the words.
2. In the middle, meditate on the combination of words and their meaning.
3. Finally, meditate on the truth of the mind.

There are three things you must not be apprehensive about:
1. Do not be apprehensive about being hungry when old.
2. Do not be apprehensive about losing support.
3. Do not be apprehensive about being despised by the world.

Six sets of four

Of the six sets of four, there are four best facts:
1. When the rope of mindfulness is uncut, it is the best meditation.
2. When cyclic existence is recognized as impermanent, it is the best recognition.
3. That which helps gain control over body and speech is the best vow.
4. That which helps flourish virtuous activities is the best retreat.

There are four "are nots":
1. If you do not refrain from negative karma, you are not a Dharma practitioner.
2. If you are devoid of monastic discipline, you are not a monk.
3. If you are devoid of commitments, you are not a tantric practitioner.
4. If you fail to let go of grasping, you are not a sublime person.

There are four roots:
1. Delighting in alcohol and women is a root of misdeeds.
2. Delighting in activities and chores is a root of distraction.
3. Grasping material wealth is a root of bondage.
4. Being a sharp tongue and quick to act is a root of negative karma.

There are four areas of error:

1. If you don't relinquish subject-object duality, you don't go beyond the surface, so this is an error.
2. If you don't relinquish the afflictions, you are a yogi in name only, so this is an error.
3. If you don't relinquish bias, your conduct is mere pretense, so this is an error.
4. If you don't let go of activities, you remain a mere ordinary person, so this is an error.

There are four resemblances:

1. Teaching Dharma to others yet failing to practice it yourself resembles a lay person playing the role of a protector in a play.
2. Selling tantra as a commodity resembles exchanging medicine for poison.
3. Failing to discipline your mind while possessing great essential instructions resembles having a jewel but remaining poor.
4. Being attached to home after having forsaken worldly norms resembles being caught in a snare after having escaped from a swamp.

There are four "musts":[56]

1. You must ensure that you do not turn your spiritual teacher into an evil friend.
2. You must ensure that you do not turn your meditation deity into a demon.
3. You must ensure that your meditation on emptiness becomes an antidote against the afflictions.

Eight sets of five

There are five difficult passages:

1. The difficult passage of cyclic existence is so hard to escape.

2. The difficult passage of discrimination is deviation from the Dharma.
3. The difficult passage of Māra is remaining self-centered and isolated.
4. The difficult passage of learning is complacency about essential instructions.
5. The difficult passage of malevolent forces is defiant conduct.

There are five misplaced things:
   1. The pursuit of learning in order to become superior to everyone else is misplaced.
   2. The giving of teachings to others in order to receive material gifts and fame is misplaced.
   3. Engagement in meditative equipoise with no instruction on meditation is misplaced.
   4. The observance of morality with an expectation of receiving material gifts and honor is misplaced.
   5. The giving of charity in order to bring everyone under your influence is misplaced.

There are five slippery slopes:
   1. If one is highly intelligent, vastly learned, and reputed to have accurate divinations, one may slide into becoming a busy preacher with no time for meditation practice.
   2. If one is sharp-minded and cares greatly for material things, one may slide into becoming a ritual master or a merchant chief.
   3. If one is powerful and has great skills, one may slide into becoming a guarantor or security [in financial transactions].
   4. If one is eloquent and quick to act, one may slide into becoming a chief or a treasurer.

5. If one remains ignorant and lacks persistence, one may slide into ordinary conduct and have no time for meditation.

There are five principal things:
1. Principal among views is the belief in the law of karma and its effects.
2. Principal among virtuous activities is restraint from harming other sentient beings.
3. Principal among meditative practices is ensuring your commitments and vows do not degenerate.
4. Principal among pledges is being able to fulfill them.
5. Principal among actions is cultivating the approximation of meditation deities.

There are five autonomies—autonomy due to:
1. Gaining mastery over the essential instructions
2. Being capable of overcoming circumstances through antidotes
3. Having awakened your natural inclinations through faith
4. Possessing an ethical discipline free of hypocrisy
5. Being capable of dispelling even the slightest harm caused by obstacles

There are five "is's":
1. If it is free of desire, this is bliss.
2. If it is free of objectification, this is emptiness.
3. If it is free of any locus, this is nonconceptuality.
4. If it is free of exertion, this is the nature of reality.
5. If desire comes to an end, this is the fruit.

There are five questions asked of Atiśa, the sole lord:
1. If one has realized the view [of emptiness], is it necessary to meditate or not?

2. To become a buddha, is it necessary to combine method and wisdom or not?
3. With regard to the bodhisattva vows, does one need to have the individual liberation (*prātimokṣa*) vows as their basis or not?
4. With regard to the wisdom-knowledge empowerment, can it be conferred by celibates above the level of upāsaka or not?[57]

There are five instances when ingesting human nourishment is not appropriate:

1. Consuming dangerous poison
2. Utilizing what was given to others
3. Enjoying a consort
4. Enjoying funds borrowed as debts
5. Consuming burning flames[58]

Six sets of six[59]

There are six types of foolishness:

1. To delight in and have affection for this mire of cyclic existence, which is the root of suffering, is foolishness.
2. To render extravagant care to this transient body, which is like a reflection, is foolishness.
3. To hoard your possessions without regard to negative karma, even if you are poor, is foolishness.
4. To pay attention to this life alone, despite the uncertainty of when the great suffering will strike, is foolishness.
5. To think you'll be able to endure the sufferings of the lower realms following death when you can't even endure the slightest suffering at present is foolishness.
6. Failing to practice the profound and vast teachings and creating suffering for yourself is foolishness.

There are six inappropriate things:

1. Not averting your thoughts from cyclic existence though aspiring to be disciplined and realized is inappropriate.
2. A fully ordained monk not practicing the Buddha's teaching; this too is inappropriate.
3. The intelligent not comprehending Dharma; this too is inappropriate.
4. The learned scholar not respecting the law of karma and its effects; this too is inappropriate.
5. The devout being soaked in negative karma; this too is inappropriate.
6. The virtuous departing to the lower realms and hells; this too is inappropriate.

There are six ways of being deluded:

1. Learning about meaningless conventional topics instead of searching for excellent instructions is deluded.
2. Building the dark dungeon of cyclic existence instead of roaming the wilderness of the mountains is deluded.
3. Lecturing on Dharma in large congregations instead of reflecting on the truth alone in solitude is deluded.
4. Being distracted by indulgence in material wealth instead of meditating in absorption on no-self is deluded.
5. Hoarding food and a wealth of avarice instead of giving charity without possessiveness is deluded.
6. Appeasing others by adhering to worldly norms instead of practicing Dharma properly is deluded.

There are six shameful things:

1. Having the gateway of sublime Dharma, which resembles a shining sun, yet performing destructive rites is indeed shameful.

2. Having taken pledges in front of the lord of the world[60] yet indulging in heedless behavior is indeed shameful.

3. Having generated the mind of supreme awakening yet denigrating others is shameful.

4. To excessively scrub and cleanse this body adorned with foul substances is shameful.

5. To be devoid of wisdom and compassion while proclaiming to be a Mahayanist is shameful.

6. Having entered the profound secret mantra yet not observing the commitments and being lazy is also shameful.

There are six recognitions:[61]

1. Recognition of the teacher as the source of mundane and supermundane higher attainments

2. Recognition of the commitments as a foundation

3. Recognition of your body as the mandala of deities

4. Recognition of sentient beings as buddhas

5. Recognition of the world of appearances and existence as like dreams and illusions

There are six perfect essential instructions:

1. Observe whether or not the enemy of the five poisons is being pacified from within.

2. Observe whether or not you are free from the illness of cyclic existence.

3. Observe whether or not you have vanquished the forces of the four māras.

4. Observe whether or not your meditative equipoise and subsequent practices are in accord.

5. Observe whether or not you are abiding in the stage of manifest movement.[62]

6. Observe whether or not you have met with the innate path.[63]

One set of seven

There is one set of seven, the seven useless things:

1. You may have taken all the vows, from going for refuge to those of secret mantra, but if you fail to avert your thoughts from worldly norms, it is useless.
2. You may regularly give teachings to others, but if your vanity is not pacified, it is useless.
3. You might show progress, but if you lose the entry-level practice of going for refuge, it is useless.
4. You might strive in virtuous activities day and night, but if they are not reinforced by the awakening mind, it is useless.
5. You may define the *imputed nature*, the *dependent nature*, and so on,[64] but if you fail to recognize things as illusion-like, it is useless.
6. You might know the three baskets of scripture, but if you lack admiration and respect for your teachers, it is useless.
7. You may meditate on emptiness, but if this does not become an antidote against affliction, it is useless.

These scattered exhortations, the essential instructions of Kharak Gomchung—instructions set down in writing by the spiritual mentor Lhopa—are complete.

5. The Sayings of Chegom

The text of this second supplement, "The Sayings of Chegom," is in fact composed of two separate short pieces. Both deal primarily with a trio, well known within the Tibetan tradition; namely, view, meditation, and action. This Master Chegom is undoubtedly Chegom Sherap Dorjé, editor of our main text, *Sayings of the Kadam Masters*. A brief biography of this master was provided at the beginning of the Sayings. Master Chegom was particularly famed for his experiential songs as well as for various pithy sayings on topics of spiritual practice. These are often organized into eighty-odd points—ten points to be remembered by beginners, eight things that one might conflate, nine nonerroneous deeds, ten potential flaws of a spiritual practitioner, five indispensable factors, seven signs of being a great being, eight practices that lead to self-imposed suffering, eight practices that constitute being kind to oneself, three perfect factors, four things that are unnecessary, and ten deeds that ensure that whatever one does becomes good.[65]

In the first of the two selections presented in this supplement, Chegom elegantly encapsulates what he sees to be the heart of the perfect view—to view all phenomena as representations of the mind, to view the mind as being empty of inherent existence, and not to have any form of attachment or grasping to this standpoint. This, Master Chegom says, is the ultimate view. Similarly, the ultimate meditation refers to placing one's mind, free of distraction, in a natural uncontrived state wherein nothing is objectified, either with respect to the outside world or the internal world of one's experience. Thirdly, the ultimate action or conduct, which emerges from a view and meditation such as this, is to act and be in the world with no judgment of rejection or affirmation, and yet to transform all adversity into the path and to have no attachment to favorable conditions. This is a vision of a life of true nonattachment. Master Chegom then goes on to envision what kind of a spiritual path will emerge from such a state of being, and what its immediate and ultimate results will be. Finally, we are reminded that in the final analysis all of these must be understood within the framework of emptiness, the ultimate nature of all things. This will ensure that we do not become stuck through grasping and instead relate to our experience and the world around us as being echo-like, dream-like, with no substantial reality to cling to.

The second text presents the same theme of view, meditation, and action from the perspective of its more graduated development under the rubric of what the master calls the "ten perfect factors." Among these ten there is a view of the initial level, of the medium level, and of the highest; a meditation of the initial, medium, and highest levels; and an action of the initial, medium, and highest levels. The final tenth factor we might see as the sign indicating success in one's practice. Thus Chegom speaks of the "progressive diminishment of self-grasping, affliction, and conceptualization" and characterizes them as a "sign of heat," which is a reference to the first stage of the path of preparation within the schema of the five stages of the path—of accumulation, preparation, seeing, meditation, and beyond training.

It's not possible, based on what little we know, to determine who might have been the compiler of these two short selections of Chegom's sayings. Nor is it possible to determine who added these two texts as an appendix to the *Sayings of the Kadam Masters*, or when they did so. Nonetheless, there are no grounds on which to dispute the attribution of these sayings to Master Chegom.

Nāmo guru!
(Homage to the teachers!)

The precious father Chegom said: "If you recognize the world of appearance and existence as the mind, realize the mind itself as empty, and have no grasping at the superiority of your realizations—this is the ultimate view.

"To be held by the glue of nondistraction, having placed your mind in the uncontrived state, and to be devoid of objectification and grasping at this or that object—this is the ultimate meditation.

"To turn adversities into the path, to sever your clinging to favorable objects, and to be devoid of adoption and rejection or affirmation and negation—this is the ultimate conduct.

"To recognize everything that occurs as devoid of substantial reality, to be devoid of rejection and acceptance with regard to good and bad, and to let go of everything at will—this is the ultimate removal of interfering forces.

"To have your perceptions dissolve into an inchoate mass, to have your delusions dismantled, and to have your clinging quickly cease—this is the ultimate sign of heat.[66]

"To be loosened from the hitching post of self-grasping, to exhaust desires through realizing everything as devoid of self-existence, and to cut the rope of expectations—this is the immediate fruit.

"On this basis, to purify your awareness, to uphold the natural ground of the dharmakāya, and to engage selflessly in the welfare of others—this is the ultimate fruit.

"Actually, even with regard to these ultimate facts, there is no ultimate enjoyment or abandonment of mind; they are ultimates only in their relative contexts.

> Therefore, since the basis is empty like an echo, do not grasp this empty echo as real.

Since the illusory path is a construct of the mind, do not, with respect to such mental constructs, engage in affirmation and negation.

Since the resultant three buddha bodies are empty names, do not, with respect to such empty names, harbor any hollow expectation or suspicion."

Nāmo guru! (Homage to the teachers!)

"The ten perfect factors are:

1. Having conviction in the law of karma and its effect is the perfect view of the initial level of mental facility.
2. Realizing all external and internal phenomena as a union of four—appearance, emptiness, awareness, and union of emptiness [and appearance]—is the perfect view of the middle level of mental facility.
3. Realizing the indivisibility of all three—the object viewed, the viewer, and the realization itself—is the perfect view of the highest level of mental faculty.
4. Abiding in a single-pointed meditative absorption is the perfect meditation of the initial level of mental facility.
5. Abiding in meditative absorption on the union of the four factors is the perfect meditation of the middle level of mental facility.
6. Abiding in the sphere of nonobjectification of the three— the object of meditation, the meditator, and the experience itself—is the perfect meditation of the highest level of mental facility.
7. Observing the law of karma and its effects as you would guard your eyes is the perfect action of the initial level of mental facility.
8. Engaging with all phenomena as if they were dreams and illusions is the perfect action of the middle level of mental facility.

9. Not engaging in anything is the perfect action of the highest level of mental facility.

10. The progressive diminishing of self-grasping, afflictions, and conceptualizations is the perfect sign of heat for all three levels of mental facility—initial, middle, and highest. These are the ten perfect factors."

These are the words of Chegom. May the welfare of sentient beings flourish.

PART II

The Book of Kadam

The *Book* and Its Spiritual Legacy

EARLIER, while identifying the Indian master Atiśa's Kadam legacy in Tibet, I spoke of the existence of a collection of a "most intriguing set of teachings" enshrined in two large volumes known together as the *Book of Kadam*.[67] The four texts selected in this second part of our volume are all drawn from this book— the first three from the volume entitled Father Teachings and the final text from Son Teachings. The volumes of the *Book* are so called because the teachings contained in the first were given in response to questions posed to Master Atiśa by "father" Dromtönpa, while the teachings in the second were given in response to questions posed by Atiśa and Drom's spiritual sons, Ngok Lekpai Sherap and Khutön Tsöndrü Yungdrung.

On one level the *Book* can be viewed as an extended commentary on Atiśa's *Bodhisattva's Jewel Garland*, a Buddhist work in twenty-six stanzas that ostensibly outline the view and practices of the bodhisattva, a buddha-to-be who dedicates his or her entire being to the altruistic ideal of bringing about others' welfare. In fact the core works of the *Book*, both the Father Teachings and Son Teachings, are framed as instructions, comments, and reflections on specific lines of *Bodhisattva's Jewel Garland*. To view the *Book* as a standard commentary on this short text, however, would miss what is unique about it. Atiśa's root text is more like a springboard or literary device used to trigger discussion of a whole host of issues pertaining to Buddhist thought and practice in Tibet. The special focus of the Father Teachings, which are framed as a series of dialogues between Atiśa and Dromtönpa, is the critical question of how to balance and integrate the foundational Mahayana Buddhist teachings with esoteric Vajrayana practices. The Son Teachings, on the other hand, are effectively tales of Dromtönpa's previous lives, akin to the *Jataka Tales* of the Buddha's previous births. They deal primarily with Dromtönpa's identification with Avalokiteśvara (the Buddha of Compassion) and the latter's supposed special affinity with Tibet.

The literary style of the first thirteen chapters of the Father Teachings, which is composed of twenty-three core chapters, consistently maintains a seven- or eight-syllable verse structure with an occasional sojourn into explanatory prose that often highlights important stages in the dialogue between Atiśa and Dromtönpa. Though they retain a strong oral flavor, these chapters contain some of the most evocative verses found in the Tibetan language. They are vibrant, immediate, poignant, and convey a profound spirituality, often tinged with a wonderful humor and irony. The verses are most evocative when addressing the ever-present theme of the illusion-like nature of reality. The use of puns, paradoxes, and other literary devices suggests that the verses are the authentic creation of a native speaker (or speakers). Each chapter ends with Dromtönpa summarizing the exchanges in a series of questions and answers, citing relevant lines from *Bodhisattva's Jewel Garland*.

The literary format for the Son Teachings is very different. Although they invoke the famous *Jātaka Tales of the Buddha*, each birth story begins with a stanza from *Bodhisattva's Jewel Garland* followed by a request by Ngok (or, in two cases, Khutön) to recount the story of a former life of Dromtönpa in relation to the cited stanza. Although written mostly in prose, the chapters often contain memorable verses as well.

A Summary of the Father and Son Teachings

The heart of the meditative practice presented in the Father Teachings is known as the the *five recollections*, an instruction encapsulated in the following verse attributed to Tārā in the *Book*:

Recall your teachers, the source of refuge;
see your body in the nature of the meditation deity;
with speech, make your mantra recitations constant;
contemplate all beings as your parents;
experience the nature of your mind as empty.
On the basis of these five factors,
make pure all roots of virtue.[68]

These five recollections unfold in the *Book* as follows: By reflecting upon the enlightened example of your teachers, profound feelings of admiration and devotion arise from your very depths such that even the hairs on your body stand on end. On this basis, you next go for refuge to the Three Jewels together with all sentient beings and ensure that you will never be separated from the practice of deity yoga, whereby you will arise as the mandalas of the four divinities—the Buddha, Avalokiteśvara, Acala, and Tārā. Then, on the basis of contemplating all beings as your kind parents, you generate the awakening mind for the benefit of these beings and abide in the meditative equipoise (*samādhi*) of the ultimate awakening mind, wherein emptiness and compassion are fused in nondual unity. In the periods subsequent to actual meditation sessions, you then cultivate the perspective of seeing all phenomena, including yourself, as illusion-like—seemingly real yet devoid of any substantiality.

At one point in the text, in the course of conversations between Atiśa and Dromtönpa on the four divinities, Dromtönpa's heart opens up and miraculously reveals progressively the

entire realm of Buddha Śākyamuni, the realm of Avalokiteśvara, the realm of Tārā, and finally the realm of the deity Acala.
It is here that we also find explicit mention of Avalokiteśvara's
famous six-syllable mantra, *Oṃ maṇi padme hūṃ*. This deity
yoga, in its developed form, came to be referred to as the practice of the *sixteen drops*. The sixteen drops are: (1) the drops
of the outer inconceivable cosmos, (2) of this earth, (3) of the
realm of Tibet, (4) of one's own immediate environment, (5)
of the deity Mother Perfection of Wisdom, (6) of Buddha
Śākyamuni, (7) of the Thousand-Armed Avalokiteśvara, (8) of
Wisdom Tārā, (9) of Tārā in her wrathful form, (10) of the
Protector Acala, (11) of Atiśa, (12) of Dromtönpa, (13) of the
vast practice of the bodhisattva, (14) of the profound view of
emptiness, (15) of the inspirational practice, and (16) of the
drop of great awakening.

The idea of the sixteen-drop practice is fairly straightforward.
Like a powerful camera lens zooming from the widest possible
angle to a progressively smaller focus, and finally to a tiny point,
the meditation becomes increasingly focused, moving from
the entire cosmos, to this world in particular, to the realm of
Tibet, to the practitioner's own dwelling, and finally culmi-
nates to one's own body. Within your body, you then visualize
the Mother Perfection of Wisdom inside your heart; within
her heart is her son, Buddha Śākyamuni; within the Buddha's
heart is the Thousand-Armed Avalokiteśvara; within his heart
is Tārā; and so on, through wrathful Tārā, Acala, Atiśa, and
Dromtönpa. Within Dromtönpa's heart you then visualize
Maitreya surrounded by masters of the lineage of vast practice.
In his heart you visualize Nāgārjuna surrounded by the masters of the lineage of profound view, and within his heart you
visualize Vajradhara surrounded by the masters of the lineage of
inspirational practice.

Finally, inside Vajradhara's heart, you visualize yourself as a
buddha, embodying all three buddha bodies, and within the

heart of yourself visualized as a buddha is a white drop the size of a mustard seed. This seed increases in size and turns into a vast radiant jewel container, at the center of which your mind is imagined as a yellow drop the size of a pea. This, in turn, increases in size and turns into an ocean of drops the color of refined gold; the ocean is transparent, smooth, resolute, vast, and pervasive, and reflects all forms. You then rest your mind, without wavering, upon this drop of great awakening, fused, and free of any sense of subject-object duality.

In the final chapter of the Father Teachings (the third selection from the *Book* in the present volume), the entire teachings are condensed into two simple practices referred to as the *two examinations*. They are (1) examining or guarding your speech when among many and (2) examining and guarding your mind when alone and are encapsulated in the following two lines from verse 23 of Atiśa's *Bodhisattva's Jewel Garland*:

Among others guard your speech;
when alone guard your mind.

In contrast to the Father Teachings within the *Book*, the Son Teachings are first and foremost a collection of birth stories of Dromtönpa's former lives as reportedly narrated by the Indian master Atiśa. Each of these birth stories is related in some way to the accounts of Dromtönpa having engaged in the practices described in the root text during his former lives. Some of these stories explicitly link the protagonist of the main story with Dromtönpa and the country of Tibet. For example, Prince Asaṅga, one of the previous incarnations of Dromtömpa, speaks the following prophetic lines in chapter 2 of the Son Teachings:

Noble one, bear witness to this:
My two parents, in the future,
in the last five-hundred-year cycle,

on the crest of snow mountains,
my father, Prabhāśrī, so-named
by the ḍākinīs of Udhyāna,
will be Drom's father, Yaksher Kushen.
My mother, the devout Satī,
will be known as Khuö Salenchikma.
I will be born on that crest of snow mountains.[69]

From the perspective of the larger Tibetan tradition, especially with regard to the myth of Avalokiteśvara's unique affinity
with the Land of Snows, chapters 5 and 19 of the birth stories
are most important. In the former, the longest chapter in the
volume by far, we find the following oft-quoted lines:

To the north of Bodhgaya, which lies in the east,
is a place called Tibet, the kingdom of Pu,
where there are sky-touching columns of towering
     mountains,
lakes of turquoise mirrors in the lowlands,
crystal stupas of white snow,
golden mounded hills of yellow grass,
incense offerings of medicinal plants,
golden flowers with vibrant colors,
and, in summer, blossoms of turquoise blue.
O Avalokiteśvara, lord of the snow mountains,
there lies your special domain;
there you shall find your devotees.[70]

Chapter 19 of the Son Teachings, the second longest chapter
of the volume, is the most elaborate in developing this theme
of Tibet as uniquely associated with Avalokiteśvara and of
Dromtönpa's place within this scheme. For example the text
tells the story of how, when Dromtönpa was born as Devarāja,
a youth prophesized that when the era of degeneration dawned

and the Buddha's teaching declined he would, at the urging of the bodhisattva Sarvanivaraṇaviśkaṃvin, take the form of a king and establish the foundation for Buddhadharma in the barbarian land of Tibet.[71] He would take birth as a king renowned as an emanation of Great Compassion Avalokiteśvara (namely, Songtsen Gampo) and would invite Tārā (the Chinese princess Wen-ch'eng) and Bhṛkuṭī (the Nepalese princess) to the central region of Tibet. He would thus transform this barbarian borderland into a central land where Dharma would flourish. The text then goes on to state that a large gathering of monks, all blessed by Dīpaṃkaraśrījñāna, would converge, and at that time people would recite the name of Avalokiteśvara and make supplications to him. They will see the emanation body of Avalokiteśvara, listen to teachings from him, and be introduced to the tantric practices related to the six-syllable mantra. In brief, great compassion would flourish so widely that the central region of Tibet would resemble the pure land of Potala.[72]

It seems that there also developed among the Kadampas a tradition of identifying Dromtönpa's three principal brother disciples with the lords of the three Buddha families and, more intriguingly, with three famous "self-arisen" icons of Avalokiteśvara.[73] One of the most interesting aspects of the nineteenth chapter is its close connection with another important Tibetan work of some antiquity that appears to have been a key text in the propagation of the tradition of identifying Tibetan imperial figures with Avalokiteśvara. This is the famous *Kakholma Testament* (literally, *Testament Extracted from a Pillar*), purportedly authored by the seventh-century Tibetan emperor Songtsen Gampo and later rediscovered as a revealed treasure text. According to a tradition dating back to the twelfth century, Atiśa is credited with having retrieved this text in Lhasa toward the end of the 1040s.[74] In fact, in the present redaction of the testament, the text opens with an interesting discussion of Atiśa's visit to the Lhasa cathedral and some miraculous visions he experienced related to the image of the self-originated Avalokiteśvara icon there. In the text's colophon Atiśa is quoted as saying that he saw the manuscript of the testament written on a blue silk cloth with gold letters and that there were three versions of the text. He is also quoted as explicitly stating that the text was discovered as a treasure in the cathedral of Lhasa.[75]

The Dalai Lamas and the Later Transmissions of the Book[76]

Like many of the sacred texts of world's great spiritual traditions, the exact origin of the *Book of Kadam*, often referred to simply as "the precious book," is difficult to determine. As already stated, the Tibetan tradition traces the source of the *Book* to a series of conversations said to have taken place between Master Atiśa and his spiritual heir Dromtönpa over a period of three years at the retreat of Yerpa. There is also a consensus in the tradition that the teachings enshrined in the *Book* were initially part of an oral transmission for at least several generations before they were written down. We do know that the current printed version of the two-volume book was finalized by Khenchen Nyima Gyaltsen in 1302, and after this, the transmission of the teachings of this special collection becomes easier to discern. A key figure in the subsequent transmission was Gendün Drup (1391– 1474), who later came to be recognized as the First Dalai Lama. The First Dalai Lama gave the transmission to Panchen Yeshé Tsemo, who passed it on to Gendün Gyatso (1476–1542), later recognized as the Second Dalai Lama. According to later historical sources, it was through the efforts of the First and Second Dalai Lamas that transmission of the *Book* became widespread in central and southern Tibet.[77]

The noted Geluk author Panchen Sönam Drakpa (1478– 1554), who was a student of the Second Dalai Lama and a tutor of the Third, states that from Gendün Drup, Mönlam Palwa received the transmission and taught it both at Ganden and Drepung, two of the largest Geluk monasteries in central Tibet.[78] Gendün Gyatso, after receiving transmission from Panchen Yeshé Tsemo, caused a great rain of the precious *Book* to fall upon many people in the Ü and Tsang provinces of central Tibet, as well as in Nyal, Dakpo, Kongpo, and many other regions far from central Tibet. Furthermore, according to the same source, the bodhisattva Lodrö Gyaltsen (1402–72) received transmission in Tsang and spread it to western Tibet. The elders Jangyalwa and Sötrepa received this transmission, the latter bringing the teaching to Yarlung.[79] That a transmission lineage of the *Book* is listed by Pema Karpo (1527–96), a principal master of the Drukpa Kagyü lineage, as well as by Taklung Ngawang Namgyal (1571–1626), one of the luminaries of the Taklung Kagyü lineage, indicates that transmission of the *Book* took place within non-Kadam and non-Geluk traditions as well.

Although the first Dalai Lamas and their immediate disciples appear to have been the primary force behind the early dissemination of the *Book* in the Geluk school, later, beginning with Panchen Losang Chögyen (1570–1662), some masters of the so-called ear-whispered teachings also took deep interest in the *Book*'s transmission, especially with regard to initiation into the sixteen drops. Among these masters was Yongzin Yeshé Gyaltsen (1713–93), who composed substantial works pertaining to the *Book* and the meditative practice of the sixteen drops. An English translation of one of these works, a lucid text in verse presenting the essential teachings of the *Book of Kadam* within the framework of Atiśa's schema of practices for the persons of three capacities—that is, the stages of the path approach—is featured in *The Book of Kadam: The Core Texts.*

Although it was only later that a systematic narrative evolved whereby the successive Dalai Lamas were cast as emanations of Avalokiteśvara—a narrative that links the Dalai Lamas with both Dromtönpa and Songtsen Gampo—the identification of

Gendün Drup with Dromtönpa was already well established shortly after his time. For example, Gendün Drup's biographer, Yeshé Tsemo, cites the translator Thukjé Palwa as stating after transmitting the *Book* to Gendün Drup, "I am a man of meritorious collection, for I have heard [the *Book*] from Drom and have now passed it on to Drom."[80] Similarly, the fifteenth-century historian of the Kadam school, Lechen Künga Gyaltsen (himself a student of Gendün Drup), states that although some say that Gendün Drup was a manifestation of Nāgārjuna and others say that he was a reincarnation of the Kadam master Neusurpa, most knew him as the emanation of Dromtönpa.[81] By the end of the sixteenth century, authors of other schools also came to refer to the First Dalai Lama as a reincarnation of Dromtönpa. Furthermore, according to some sources, the First Dalai Lama's family hailed from the same ancestral lineage as Dromtönpa's. When Gendün Gyatso was formally recognized as the reincarnation of Gendün Drup, the connection was naturally formed between the Second Dalai Lama and Dromtönpa and, through this relationship, to Avalokiteśvara himself.

It was the Great Fifth, however, who created the edifice of the mytho-religious worldview in which the institution of the Dalai Lamas came to have a significance far greater than that of successive reincarnations of the important historical figure Gendün Drup. The Great Fifth and his ingenious regent, Desi Sangyé Gyatso (1653–1705), brought about a creative marriage of the two textual sources for the narrative of Avalokiteśvara's direct intervention in the unfolding fate of the land of Tibet and its people.[82] Both the *Kakholma Testament* and Dromtönpa's birth stories in the *Book of Kadam* were already recognized as possessing some mysterious background, one a revealed treasure text and the other literally a "miraculous volume." In his influential *Yellow Beryl: A History of the Ganden Tradition*, Desi Sangyé Gyatso, in addition to providing copious citations from scripture, interweaves beautifully evocative quotes from the *Book of Kadam* and the *Kakholma Testament* to explicitly identify the Great Fifth with Songtsen Gampo, Dromtönpa, the treasure revealer Nyangral Nyima Öser (1124–92), Ngari Panchen (1487–1542), and especially the preceding Dalai Lamas— Gendün Drup, Gendün Gyatso, and Sönam Gyatso.[83] Through efforts like this, the Great Fifth and his regent integrated the myth of Avalokiteśvara's compassionate manifestation throughout the ages as spiritual teachers and rulers of the Land of Snows into a concrete institution that Tibetans could nurture, preserve, and cherish. For Tibetans, the mythic narrative that began with Avalokiteśvara's embodiment in the form of Songtsen Gampo in the seventh century—or even earlier with the mytho-historical figures of the first king of Tibet, Nyatri Tsenpo (traditionally calculated to have lived around the fifth century B.C.E.), and Lha Thothori Nyentsen (ca. third century C.E.), during whose reign some sacred Buddhist scriptures are believed to have arrived in Tibet—and continued with Dromtönpa in the eleventh century continues today in the person of His Holiness Tenzin Gyatso, the Fourteenth Dalai Lama.

Perhaps the most important legacy of the *Book*, at least for the Tibetan people as a whole, is that it laid the foundation for the later identification of Avalokiteśvara with the lineage of the Dalai Lamas, who continually enact the solemn pledge of that compassionate deity to accord special care for the people of the Land of Snows.[84] Although Avalokiteśvara was propitiated in Tibet before the tenth century, and although the designation of the seventh-century Tibetan emperor Songtsen Gampo as an embodiment of Avalokiteśvara most probably predates Atiśa's arrival in Tibet, the available textual evidence points strongly toward the eleventh and twelfth centuries as the period during which the full myth of Avalokiteśvara's special destiny with Tibet came to take shape. During this era the belief that this compassionate spirit intervenes in the fate of the Tibetan people by manifesting as benevolent rulers and teachers took firm root. It is also becoming increasingly clear that Atiśa played a crucial role in the propagation, if not development, of the key elements of these myths.[85] The story of the *Book of Kadam* is part of that overall story, one that indelibly shaped the self-identity of the Tibetan people and their understanding of Tibet's place in the world.

THE FATHER TEACHINGS

THE FOLLOWING three texts are chapters 6, 14, and 23 of the Father Teachings, the heart of the first volume of the two-volume *Book of Kadam*. The entire twenty-three-chapter work—translated in *The Book of Kadam: The Core Texts*—is known more specifically by the name *Jewel Garland of Dialogues*, which explicitly highlights the dialogical nature of the text. These "dialogues" are drawn from a series of conversations between the two founding fathers of the Kadam tradition—Master Atiśa and his spiritual heir Dromtönpa—that are thought to have taken place at the retreat of Nyethang Or in central Tibet sometime in the eleventh century.

The dialogues begin with a lengthy preamble that sets the context for the conversations. Part of this scene setting involves describing a mystical dimension wherein Master Atiśa is seen as sitting inside a rainbow pavilion on the right leg of goddess Tārā, as the retreat of Yerpa takes on the form of Potala, Avalokiteśvara's heavenly abode. In this form Master Atiśa is surrounded by enlightened beings, such as buddhas and bodhisattvas, a congregation that also includes Dromtönpa. The text then proceeds to enumerate the various enlightened qualities of Master Drom, including how he had in his previous lives fulfilled the needs of people in the Land of Snows. The text also speaks of how Drom had at present assumed a particular existence in a family of nomads to help fulfill certain specific aims.[86] These descriptions of the transcendent context are then followed by descriptions grounded in the current context, which underline some of the unique qualities of Drom the man, especially his celebrated humility.

Finally, the preamble presents Dromönpa as making an appeal to Master Atiśa with the following lines: "At this moment, when the omniscient one is still alive, I can cut the rope of doubts pertaining to good and evil. Due to the force of the negative karma of your potential trainees, the conqueror could depart to other realms. Should this happen, it will be difficult for me to request teachings." He then goes on to speak of how people of the degenerate era possess untamed temperaments and of how, even when they receive teachings, they fail to practice. "So at this time I would like to request a teaching that most paragons of virtue who will appear after me will be able to rely upon. . . ." In response, Master Atiśa states, among other things, the following:

My mindstream is enriched by the teachings;
all these teachings possess scriptural authority.
How the transmission of these scriptures flow
I shall reveal to the intelligent, both directly and indirectly.
Merely hearing it will bring satisfaction.

Thus begins the *Jewel Garland of Dialogues*, which runs over three hundred pages.

The Three Selected Texts

The three texts selected for our volume from the Father Teachings—chapters 4, 16, and 23—all represent in one way or another meditations on the nature of our mind. The first, "How All Blames Lies in a Single Point," echoes a famous line attributed to Master Atiśa and found in the *Seven-Point Mind Training*:

Banish all blames to the single source.
Toward all beings contemplate their great kindness.[87]

Ostensibly, the text begins with Drom requesting Master Atiśa to explain the well-known Buddhist teaching on the twelve links of dependent origination. Atiśa defers the actual explanation of the twelve links to a later occasion and, cutting to the chase, speaks about the true root of all bondage—grasping at self. This then opens up an exchange between Atiśa and Drom about the exact nature of what this self-grasping might be. As the difficulty of pinpointing what exactly this self-grasping is becomes increasingly evident, Drom is reminded of not only the ubiquitous nature of this self-grasping but also that it resides within each one of us—it is in fact part of our mind-stream. This grasping manifests in such forms as our instinctive desire to seek for ourselves what is good while leaving what is bad to others and in our manifold experiences of attachment and aversion.

The conversations then take the reader through a penetrating inquiry into the nature of the mind that is the domain of self-grasping, afflictions, and so on. The mind, being devoid of color and shape and having no audible, olfactory, gustatory, or tactile qualities, is found to be beyond the realm of the material. Deeper contemplation reveals that actually everything we perceive is a construct of our own mind. This awareness of all appearances as expressions of the mind and mind itself being empty, a mere absence, offers a powerful antidote—a perspective of perfect equanimity—toward all the things that ordinarily afflict us. Interestingly, Master Atiśa takes this insight into the emptiness of all things to be naturally opening the individual practitioner to the realm of altruistic outlook and way of life, especially the cultivation of awakening mind, *bodhicitta*.

The next chapter from the Father Teachings, "Cutting the Root of Suffering," begins with an explicit change of tone and voice: "Now the time has come to speak in plain vernacular Tibetan." It then proceeds through a series of rapid verbal exchanges back and forth between Atiśa and Dromtönpa. Most of these exchanges are one-line sentences, a style maintained in this and the immediately succeeding chapter of the *Book*. Here, Atiśa identifies negative karma to be the root of our suffering, and such karma in turn is seen as arising from our notions of a self conceived on the basis of our aggregates, our body and mind. In probing the ways in which the notion of self gives rise to various afflictions—conceit, attachment, aversion—which then lead to the creation of negative karma, Atiśa and Drom then engage in a series of exchanges riddled with wordplay and humor, including the revelation of paradoxes in seemingly straightforward conventional statements. The exchanges between the two masters become so riveting that, at one point in the narrative, the goddess Tārā makes an appearance, exclaiming, "Exchanging jokes is an indication of great thirst. I, too, have heard of your love of humor, which seems to be true. I have therefore come to listen."

The text then moves to a discussion on how to deal with our uncontrolled habitual thoughts, which distract us and obstruct us from being able to rest our mind in its natural state of equilibrium. Here Atiśa invokes the name of one of his tantric gurus, Avadhūti, and presents the instruction he received from this master on how to "level out our conceptions." This well-known teaching is more formally presented in a short work entitled *Leveling Out All Conceptions* and can be found in *Mind Training: The Great Collection*. The final section of this chapter on "Cutting the Root of Suffering" deals with how to counter the excitation and laxity that arise when we are meditating, these two being the key obstructions to meditative stability.

Our third and final text is in fact the final chapter of the Father Teachings and is presented in the *Book* also as a concluding summary of the entire dialogue series. It opens with the following appeal from Drom: "This treatise encompassing such vast themes is extremely difficult. So please teach us, now, a profound practice that summarizes all the points." Entitled "The Two Examinations," the chapter elaborates on the following lines from the *Bodhisattva's Jewel Garland*:

Among others guard your speech;
when alone guard your mind.

The instructions on the first of these two examinations essentially involves bringing constant awareness to our speech: the various forms of speech—hurtful, deceiving, senseless, and so on—the motives behind our speech, and knowing the appropriate time and situation to say things. What is presented is a powerful illustration of how an individual can bring self-knowledge into everyday life, thus ensuring a mindful life characterized by sound discipline.

In the second examination, Master Atiśa leads us through a series of contemplations on the nature of mind and its intriguing "unfindable" nature. There is even an admission that, when it comes to verbalizing what exactly mind is, even the fully enlightened buddhas come to a pause. The chapter ends with a dedication, effectively concluding the dialogue series that constitutes the Father Teachings.

6. How All Blame Lies in a Single Point

ON ANOTHER OCCASION when father Atiśa and his son were staying at their residence at Nyethang Or, Drom prostrated to Atiśa and, recollecting the method of sustaining the mind and so forth, stated:

"Ignorance, craving, and grasping are the causes of sentient beings. Volition and becoming serve as their conditions, while their effects are consciousness, name and form, the six sense fields, contact, feelings, birth, and aging and death.[88] So it is these three—causes, conditions, and effects—that alone turn the wheel of impurity throughout the universe. Covering all our own defects with our palms, we unearth all the frailties of others with our fingers. Students do not implement the teacher's words, and sons do not listen to what their fathers tell them. O great Atiśa, a negative era has dawned. Although sentient beings share the experience of the impure chain of the twelve links of dependent origination, the beings of this degenerate era are partaking individually in what is a common resource. Since it could potentially benefit one or two future trainees, I request you to give a brief explanation of the twelve links of dependent origination."

Atiśa replied, "I will explain this later when we have to lift our robes above the mire."

"In that case, what is the root of bondage?" asked Drom.

Atiśa: "It is the grasping at self."

"What is this grasping at self?" enquired Drom.

"It is something that wants all positive qualities for oneself alone and wants others alone to take on all misfortune."

"Then please explain it in such a manner that we can say 'This is self-grasping,'" asked Drom.

Atiśa replied: "Where would one find something of which it could be said that 'This is the reified self-grasping?'"

"In that case, please explain to me how it is that this self-grasping wants everything and transfers all blames onto others."

Atiśa replied, "Upāsaka, why even ask me? It is pervasive in sentient beings. You know this, so what need is there to ask? Even so, I have also seen attachment and aversion labeled as self-grasping."

"Atiśa, there are people who possess such forms of grasping?"

"Where do they exist?" responded Atiśa.

"They are within one's own mental continuum," replied Drom.

"Upāsaka, what is one's own mental continuum?"

"It is that which wants and grasps at everything," replied Drom.

Atiśa: "I would say the same."

"Where does this self-grasping reside?" inquired Drom.

"It is devoid of parts, and I have never seen it myself. There is nothing that abides where there is nowhere to abide. I do not know the colors and shapes of something with no reality," replied Atiśa.

Drom then asked, "If this is so, how can something so feeble exist?"

Atiśa responded, "Can't one perceive mirage water, a double moon, dream horses and elephants, and so on?"

"Master, these are delusions."

Atiśa said, "I accept this to be so. It is not that he, self-grasping, indulges in attachment and aversion on the basis of it being existent. Dogs bark in the wilderness because of an empty container, and our mindstream is greatly perturbed with no ground at all."

"Master, if such are the examples, self-grasping seems to be something that never existed at all," said Drom.

"What is this thing that 'seems to be'? It must be real."

"Master, in that case, do the forms and functions of the abyss of the three lower realms, the qualities of the higher realms, and the ethical norms of affirmation and rejection also exist?"

"There is a dreamer of dreams. Isn't there?" Atiśa responded.

"Master, it is not the same. Dreams are not created by oneself. Though false, they arise [spontaneously]. Birth in the higher realms, lower realms, and the ethical norms of affirmation and rejection were created."

"Who created them?" asked Atiśa.

"They were created by the mind," replied Drom.

"I would say the same. Dreams are also created by the mind, Upāsaka, for if not by the mind, who creates them? Does some other thing create them? For were they not created by something else or by the mind, Upāsaka, then you have lied about what is itself a lie. The objects of dreams are false; they are devoid of all characterizations such as self, other, and so on. In the same manner, even the ethical norms of affirmation and rejection, such as [the causes for taking birth in] the lower realms and so on, are conjured by the mind itself, which then does the affirming and rejecting."

"If this is so, is self-grasping the root of attachment and aversion, and is this one's own mind?" asked Drom.

"What is the color of the mind?" asked Atiśa.

"I have never seen it."

"Then what kind of shape does it have?" asked Atiśa.

"Master, I have never seen it."

"Since it exists with neither color nor shape, and also since it has never been seen with the eyes, this indicates that it does not exist as a form. So empty it of physicality and set it aside. Upāsaka, what type of sound does it have, melodious or unmelodious, loud or muffled?"

"Master, I have never heard it before," replied Drom.

"So since it does not appear as melodious or unmelodious, loud or muffled, and so on, it is not heard by the ears. Given that if it does exist [as sound], it should be audible to the ears, and [given that it is not heard], it does not exist. Now that the mind is devoid also of sound, set it aside. Upāsaka, what type of smell does it have, fragrant or unfragrant?"

"Master, I have never smelled an odor of the mind or mind itself," replied Drom.

"Drom, had it an odor, there is no doubt it would have been smelled by the nose. Given that it has never been smelled, this indicates that the mind is devoid of smell. So set aside this emptiness that is the absence of smell. Drom, does your mind exist as some kind of taste, be it delicious or unsavory?"

"All sorts of things seem to emerge from the master's speech. How can there be a norm[89] for distinguishing between delicious and unsavory on the basis of tasting the mind?" exclaimed Drom.

"Drom, in that case, does the mind not exist?"

"Master, how can there be the eating of mind, and how can there be the tasting of mind?" asked Drom.

"Drom, this indicates that your mind is not a taste. For if it were a taste, the tongue would experience it. As it is not experienced by the tongue, this indicates that it is not a taste. So set aside that which is devoid also of taste. Drom, what kind of tactile quality does the mind have, soft or coarse?"

"Master, I have never seen the tactile quality of the mind," he replied.

"Drom, why is this so?"

"There is no norm pertaining to observing the tactile quality of the mind," replied Drom.

Atiśa then responded: "Normlessness abounds in sentient beings that are wild. Given that the mind is not an object of tactile experience, this is an indication that it is devoid of tactile quality. So set aside the mind that is also not a tactile phenomenon. Drom, what kind of things exist as objects of mental consciousness?"

"Master, in order for something to appear as an object of mental consciousness, it seems that the senses need to have an immediately preceding condition. For without first becoming the object of the senses, there is no immediately preceding condition that is the object of mental consciousness."

"Fabrications of conceptualization can appear too," responded Atiśa.

"Master, even fabrications are preceded by their propensities. Furthermore, isn't the entailment 'because something is not an object of the five senses, it does not exist as any of the five sense objects' a little too sweeping?"

"Upāsaka, what are you saying? I have not listed all objects to be within these [five sense objects]. I have only listed your mind in addition to these sense objects. For if the mind exists as any of these, then when you observe it, it should exist as a form, be heard as a sound, and so on. Since it is not perceived as any of these, where does the mind reside? Upāsaka, even ordinary mundane people would give up and shake their hands and exclaim 'I have never seen such a thing with my eyes, nor have I heard it with my ears. I have never smelled its odor, never tasted its flavor, nor does it exist anywhere within the sphere of mental consciousness.' You, on the other hand, are a person who has been ripened by the pith instructions of the sublime teachers, in whose heart the higher attainments of the meditation deities have entered, and a person who practices the three baskets of scripture in one sitting. So you of all people should not add meaningless branches and leaves [onto a nonexistent tree].

"All of this is the mind. I have realized this nature of mind, for I am a son of Avadhūti. Now even if one's faults are exposed, it is the mind. Even if one is praised, it is the mind. Whether happy or sad, it is the mind. Given that all of these are equal in being the mind, whatever defects arise in your mental continuum wherein self is perceived when there is no self, crush them and let go of them. There is no point in concealing such unestablished defects inside a cave that is itself not established. There is no point in turning these into poisons and causing illness. There is no reason that the number of illnesses should remain fixed at five. There is no need for these to sever the life of liberation and cast one into the three lower realms. Although dreams are unreal, it serves no purpose to dream of suffering.

"Drom, cast out all these false defects. If the sign of having cleansed these defects is positive, this is fine; if it is not, this is fine too. Within this equality of everything being appearances of an unreal mind, if others are delighted when praised, then praise them. Do not seek out another's faults, for there is no searcher within you. If something is to be concealed at all, conceal your own higher qualities. The time has now come for this. If something is to be proclaimed at all, proclaim the higher qualities of others. Others, delighted, will not accumulate negative karma on the basis of you. This also has the benefit of dislodging the foundation stones of the afflictions, such as attachment and aversion. Whatever good qualities exist in others, seek out each of them individually and reveal them. Upāsaka, now do you understand how everything is the mind?"

"Yes, I do," replied Drom.

"In that case, do you understand the mind's true mode of being?"

"Yes, I do," replied Drom.

Atiśa: "So what need is there of desires for this mind; cultivate contentment. Even though you perceive many sentient beings, all of them are your fathers and mothers who have taken joy in your overcoming of misfortune and attainment of good fortune. They have cleaned your runny nose with their mouths, your excrement with their hands, have nurtured you with kingdoms and with gifts, and some, despite having been abandoned by us, have cared for us again. It is due to the kindness of the teacher that positive qualities are revealed. In general, it is the teacher who has done you the great kindness of granting you your ultimate aim. And it is your parents who are the source of great kindness granting you joy and happiness in this life. You should therefore recognize their kindness and repay their kindness.

"For this, serve the teacher through respectful veneration and meditative practice, and toward your parents, in order to repay their kindness, cultivate immeasurable loving-kindness, immeasurable compassion, immeasurable joy when they are happy, and immeasurable equanimity that is free of discriminating thoughts of near and far. For the benefit of all—all your mothers—strive as much as possible to attain buddhahood and, discarding lingering doubts, cherish your persistence in meditative practice. Abandoning all obstacles such as sloth, mental dullness, and laziness, endeavor with joyful perseverance.

"Drom, although we speak of 'recognizing the kindness of others and repaying it,' it all seems to come down to the practice of the four immeasurable thoughts, such as loving-kindness and compassion; the stabilization of the awakening mind; its enhancement from high to ever higher levels; and the definite steering of one's parents with the paddles of [the two awakening minds,] aspiring and engaging. So this [recognizing others' kindness and repaying it] refers to a cousin of desire, whereby one has relinquished self-centeredness and generates kindheartedness desiring one's parents' happiness and desiring to repay their kindness."

Drom replied:

"Though the master has given many excellent teachings,
If summarized, it is this:

> Reveal your own shortcomings,
> but do not seek out others' errors.
> Conceal your own good qualities,
> but proclaim those of others.
>
> Forsake gifts and ministrations;
> at all times relinquish gain and fame.
> Have modest desires, be easily satisfied,
> and reciprocate kindness.
>
> Cultivate love and compassion,
> and stabilize your awakening mind.[90]

"There is nothing other than this."

Atiśa responded, "Yes, this is so. When properly condensed, [my teachings] are encompassed in these lines."

This concludes the sixth chapter from the *Jewel Garland of Dialogues*, "How All Blame Lies in a Single Point."

7. Cutting the Root of Suffering

ONCE AGAIN, at that very same place and in the presence of the teacher endowed with the qualities [described earlier], our teacher Drom Gyalwai Jungné spoke:

"Listen, wise one. The people of Tibet need to be tamed. As such, the time has come for me to appeal to you in Tibet's own language—a language that is effective and rich in the vernacular of the uneducated—and in words whose meanings are comprehended the moment one hears them. What is the root of suffering?"

Atiśa replied, "Drom, it is negative karma."

"Master, what is the root of negative karma?"

"Drom, it is the aggregates, the 'I,' or the self."

"Master, now how does the 'I' or the self act as the root of negative karma?"

"Drom, it is by needing everything."

"Master, how does it need everything?"

"It wants oneself to be superior and others to be inferior," Atiśa replied.

"Master, how should one refer to this?"

"Drom, it should be referred to as 'attachment and aversion ridden.'"

"Master, in whom is this strongest?"

"Drom, it is strongest in those whose spiritual practice is weak but whose conceit is strong."

"Master, doesn't one become conceited because one has something?"

"Drom, fireflies feel that there are no lights other than their own."

"Master, in their case, too, aren't they conceited because they do possess a flash of light?"

"Drom, the sun and moon are never conceited."

"In that case, Master, will conceit lead to success on the path or not?"

"Drom, if one is conceited with the thought 'I will definitely succeed if I work for others' welfare,' this will lead to success on the path. Drom, if one is conceited with the thought 'I will definitely understand if I pursue the training,' this will lead to success on the path. If one is conceited with the thought 'I will definitely be capable if I observe ethical discipline,' this will lead to success on the path."

"Master, I wonder if all of these are genuine conceitedness."

"Drom, I am not saying that they are."

"Master, are there forms of conceitedness that do not have its full characteristics?"

"Drom, what kinds of defining characteristics do you need?"

"Master, I seek a definition that can illustrate the definiendum upon its basis."

"Keep quiet, Drom; for if we were to do that, it would not lead to success on the path. That which leads to success on the path is a similitude of conceit."

"Master, are you speaking of a similitude leading to success on the path?"

"In that case, Drom, does not a similitude lead to success on the path?"

"Master, where is there a similitude leading to success on the path?"

"Drom, all instances in dreams of the recognition that all phenomena are dream-like are cases in point."

"Master, this is, in fact, what is called genuine. Merely knowing that heat is the defining character of fire does not lead in any way to success on the path."

"Drom, is heat not the defining character of fire?"

"Master, in that case are all phenomena permanent and substantially real?"

"Drom, this is not the same. As for being permanent and substantially real, there is no basis."

"Master, so heat being the defining character of fire is real because of having a basis?"

"Drom, you are indeed sharp with words."

"Master, in that case is it fire?"

"Drom, what else would it be?"

"Master, you accept that heat is the defining character of fire."

"Drom, this seems like an instance of knowing something substantially real."

"Master, since there has never been a substantial reality, the only possibility is that it is similar to a substantial reality."

"Drom, are you not being conceited here?"

"Master, if mere imputations can lead to success on the path, being conceited is okay."

"Drom, is this a sense of superiority or not?"

"Master, is a sense of superiority an object to be abandoned or not?"

"Drom, if one clings, it is an object to be abandoned."

"Master, if one does not cling, is it then not an object to be abandoned?"

"Drom, a sense of superiority without clinging is a mere similitude."

"Master, how should one deal with a sense of superiority with clinging?"

"Drom, level conceitedness flat."

"Master, what methods are there for this?"

"Drom, recollect the pith instructions of teachers who have practical experience."

"Master, what are such teachers' instructions?"

"Drom, having taught you ever since the universe began, you are now asking for a teacher's instruction?!"

"Master, we have associated with each other since the beginning of the universe, yet we are still together, aren't we?"

"Drom, that was a joke."

"Master, your repartee is as hot as fire."

"Drom, as an answer it is red [hot]."

"Master, if it is timely, it is the right answer."

"Drom, in your case, is there such a thing as timely?"

"Master, I am not a sky flower."

"Drom, in that case, who are you?"

"Master, what is the color of white?"

"Drom, you are an expert in waiting for the critical moment."

"Master, he who is expert in waiting for the critical moment is learned."

"Drom, a learned one is quite busy."

"Master, why is this so?"

"Drom, this is because he has to wait for all the critical moments."

"Master, regardless of whether this is so, rushing about is being busy."

The master laughed and said, "Like you Tibetans?"

"Master, just like an Indian mendicant."

"Drom, he bites each grain of rice."

"Master, this will make the rice the appropriate coarseness."

As Drom spoke these words, a green lady carrying a vase filled with wisdom nectar poured nectar into two crystal ladles—one white and the other yellow—and offered them to Atiśa and his son. She said, "Exchanging jokes is an indication of great thirst.

I, too, have heard of your love of humor, which seems to be true. I have therefore come to listen."

Drom replied, "Lady, are you also a mendicant? Hé! Hé! You had to wander in all the directions accompanying a white youth."[91]

Atiśa inquired, "Why did the white youth experience such haste?"

"Master, he had far too many mothers. Sometimes he was distracted by joy and happiness because they were too happy. Sometimes he had to vigilantly look after them because they were suffering so much."

"How many were there?" asked Atiśa.

"Master, it would be good if there were numbers and limits, but there are none."

"Lady, is space not the limit?" asked Atiśa.

"Master, you measure space then," asked the lady.

Atiśa replied, "I do not know. Ask Drom; he is good at traveling around. He also loves making things elaborate and brief. Also, there must be a limit to space that one can speak of."

"What kind of elaboration and abbreviation do I engage in?" asked Drom.

"Drom, you engage in elaborations about the size of space."

"Master, you have the thought that I do, so please show us the limit of space."

"Drom, what are you talking about? I have never measured space."

"Master is telling a sudden lie. Having said that Drom engages in elaborations about the size of space, you are now claiming that you have never measured space."

"Drom, I said that you engage in elaborations about the size of space, but I did not say that so much is the size of space."

"Master, if you say that Drom engages in elaborations about the size of space, when this analogy is related to the actual fact, you must know both the analogy and fact you compared it to. It is strange that you, a learned man, would make such correlations."

"Drom, you may be right this time. However, if to say that something were equal to space, one had to comprehend [the limits of] space itself, there would be none who could use space as an analogy."

"Master, is this not a case of doing something while being ignorant? An intelligence that discovers the limit of space is difficult to find indeed."

"Drom, who has measured that space-like ultimate nature of all phenomena?"

"Master, here something measureless is used as an analogy. If space has a measure, it is not an appropriate analogy."

"Drom, how joyful it would be if I were surrounded by people like you who have no conceit and are learned in Dharma."

"Master, this would be of no benefit. Instead, it would be far more joyful if all sentient beings became human beings like me and were here in your presence to partake exclusively in the Mahayana teachings. However, as with attaining buddhahood on the basis of a female body, this seems to be rare."

As Drom made this statement, the blue-green lady appeared vividly in the form of a tathāgatha. Master Atiśa laughed and exclaimed, "What you have illuminated directly for us is an excellent form indeed!"

"One who has already become fully enlightened can display any form, both excellent and inferior. I was speaking of women who possess the fetters of the afflictions."

Then the goddess returned to her own form and asked, "Great Compassion, whose afflictions are greater, mine or those of a woman with the fetters of the afflictions? I, for one, carry the afflictions of all sentient beings, while a woman who is fettered carries only her own share. Without relinquishing the afflictions, one does not become fully enlightened, yet the afflictions are so extensive."

"In that case," replied Drom, "I, too, am greatly afflicted, for I am carrying space."

"Drom, there is nothing to carry of space," responded Tārā.

"Tārā, there is no carrier either, so cast away everything into equanimity," said Drom.

"Who is it that carries the afflictions?" Drom asked Atiśa.

"Drom, whoever possesses self-grasping."

"In that case, Tārā does not have self-grasping, for she is liberated. As for we who possess self-grasping, how can we relinquish it?"

"Drom, how many times does conceptualization occur in a single day?"

"Master, conceptualization occurs an inconceivable number of times."

"Drom, how often does the realization of the ultimate expanse arise?"

"Master, being overwhelmed by conceptions, it does not appear to arise."

"For this, Drom, you need the standpoint of my teacher Avadhūtipa."[92]

"Master, do reveal to us that instruction of your teacher."

"Drom, one transforms whatever conceptions arise into reality."

"Master, if all logs turn into gold, this would be exactly what those with greed need. But how can such a transformation be brought about?"

"Drom, it is how, on the basis of pith instructions, a base metal is transformed into gold by utilizing the alchemist's elixir. One needs to understand the essential point of the method."

"Do reveal to us the essential point, Master."

"To defeat the enemy, Drom, first you must recognize the enemy."

"What is the enemy?"

"It is conceptualization, Drom."

"How does one destroy that?"

"Drom, destroy it the moment it surfaces."

"How should one proceed to destroy it?"

"Drom, observe where its base is; analyze its shape, color, and so on, and examine its past, future, and so on. Seek where it goes to and where it comes from. At that time, it will not be found."

"Why is this so?"

"It cannot be found because it never was, Drom."

"When it is not found, what should one do then?"

"Drom, this is called 'transforming conception into the ultimate expanse.' If it cannot be found when searched for, this is a sign that it is the ultimate expanse, so place your mind at rest upon this."

"What if it arises again?"

"Then level it out again, Drom."

"Can one skillfully deal with this in a gradual manner?"

"Drom, this wouldn't work, so destroy it by beating it with the antidotes."[93]

"Are there any other objects to be abandoned?"

"Drom, harbor no excessive thoughts; concentrate entirely all your aspirations into one."

"Are there other paths or not?"

"A two-forked road will not take you far, Drom, so let go and be single-pointed in your path."

"Are there other aspirations or not?"

"Drom, if you have too many aspirations, you will lose the actual purpose. Do not initiate too many tasks; let go and be single-pointed in your decision."

"Though this is true, nevertheless when adverse conditions happen, such as sickness, it is difficult."

"Drom, what are you saying? There is no better spiritual teacher than these."

"Are they spiritual teachers or what? They are sent by a malevolent force!"

"Why do you say this? Where can one find more excellent buddhas than these?"

"A buddha? But it brings such acute pain?"

"You did not understand, Drom. Sickness is a great broom for negative karma and defilements."

"I can't say whether it is a broom for cleansing negative karma and defilements, but I do know it brings great suffering."

"Drom, with respect to this, too, when you do not find it as you search for it repeatedly, then the great manifestation of the ultimate expanse rises."

"In that case, should I be happy when suffering befalls me?"

"Drom, if you are to undertake a genuine Dharma practice, press down on the lid of your happiness-desiring thoughts."

"A cycle of suffering is bound to come."

"Drom, by enduring great hardship, connect suffering with suffering."

"I seek to do this to its end."

"Drom, when you connect them, they get disconnected; this is the essential point."

"Why is this so?"

"This is so, Drom, because one suffers by repeatedly desiring only happiness."

"How should one conduct oneself, Master, if one were to summarize all the points?"

"Since self is the root of all negative karma, discard it entirely, like the corpse of one's dead father."

"Master, what objects are to be affirmed?"

"Since helping others is the source of enlightenment, like finding a wish-granting jewel, uphold and embrace it."

"Master, aren't there things that should be left neutral in equanimity?"

"Since both self and others are unborn, let go and discard them with ease in the expanse of the equanimity of nonarising."

"In that case, you accept that. Master, what is the root of affliction that must be relinquished?"

"It is this great conceptualization."

"Master, what is the method of destroying this?"

"None other than leveling it out, Drom."

"Master, how is it relinquished by means of its antidote?"

"By means of beating it with no hesitation whatsoever. All paths are traversed by means of this single path, too, and all aspirations are concentrated into this single one. Since sickness and so on motivates one to perform spiritual practice, they can compel one to engage in Dharma practice. Therefore they are excellent spiritual teachers. They reveal the dangers of adverse conditions, such as malevolent forces, thus allowing us to see those who show us how to avert such dangers as buddhas.

"It is difficult for ordinary beings to see all the buddhas, Drom.

"Drom, this is all like a mother who disciplines her son and leads him to goodness. True renunciation will arise within, and we will remember the excellent Dharma. We will be closer to the buddhas in heart, so this is excellent," the master said.

"Drom, if one takes on the sickness of all sentient beings every time one is ill, there is no opportunity for negative action and defilement to defeat a great hero. Drom, every time suffering arises, banish the blame to self-grasping, and when you search for that suffering, you will not find it. Drom, if a hundred conceptualizations, such as concepts of suffering, occur because one searches for them one hundred times, one will not find them one hundred times. Finding the truth of not finding is the ultimate expanse. In this respect, my teacher Avadhūtipa stated:

> The nature of conceptualization is the ultimate expanse;
> when they arise, it is joyful, for they are an excellent
>   impetus.
> Of what use are they, since they cannot be found?
> They are but the effulgence of the ultimate mode of being.

"Drom, the intentions of all the buddhas are found in him. I, too, feel thus:

> Even in a single day, within the realm of self-grasping,
> hundreds of thoughts occur, useful and useless;
> the instant they arise, I search for their antidotes.
> Since I do not find them, they seem to be the ultimate
>   expanse alone.
>
> For if they do exist, out of the great multitude of instances,
> is there a rule that states that not even a single one should
>   be found?"

Drom responded, "Today our conversation has been most enjoyable. The appearance of the goddess has also warmed the teacher's heart, and the teacher's instructions were most profound."

This is the collection on how to recollect the teacher's instructions when conceit and thoughts of superiority arise.

Again, Drom asked: "If this mind becomes too dejected, Teacher, how should one illuminate it?"

"Set it astride the cool blowing wind."

"Master, what should one do once one has set it thus astride?"

"Drom, given the multitude of animals, the attainment of a human life is joyful."

"How should one practice after generating such a thought?"

"Drom, obtaining it is not adequate, for it disintegrates easily."

"What methods can be applied in light of this?"

"Drom, collect the golden flowers of ethical discipline."

"Where should such a person seek shelter?"

"Drom, seek it in the ocean of uncontaminated teachings."

"How does one abide in such an ocean?"

"Drom, abide by consuming rose apple juice and gold."

"I am not asking about how to eat."

"Drom, how can one abide without the resources?"

"One consumes meditative absorption."

"Drom, there is no greater food than this."

"How does this help against dejection?"

"Drom, one will think, 'How joyful it is that such things will happen.'"

"What is joyful about this?"

"Drom, it is so because one's ultimate aspiration comes about."

"On what basis does dejection arise?"

"Drom, it does so when conditions for negativity are created by others."

"How can the conditions for negativity be dispelled?"

"Drom, think, 'They are an impetus for practicing forbearance.'"

"What benefits are there in practicing forbearance?"

"Drom, if one aspires for an attractive appearance, forbearance is indispensable."

"How does forbearance lead to physical attractiveness?"

"Drom, [the body endowed with] the exemplary signs and the noble marks."

"Apart from this, is anything else achieved from it?"

"Drom, one also attains speech endowed with sixty qualities of perfect melody."

"The method for dispelling dejection is most excellent. Master, do both mental excitement and laxity arise?"

"Drom, they are in abundance in those who are unruly."

"What methods should one pursue to dispel these?"

"Drom, there is none greater than perfect equanimity."

"What happens if one meditates on compassion?"

"Drom, they can arise, for one can feel dejected."

"Should one meditate on loving-kindness alone?"

"Drom, here, too, dejection can arise."

"Should one meditate on joy alone?"

"Drom, here, too, dejection can arise."

"In that case, should one cultivate equanimity?"

"Drom, here, too, delusion can arise."

"Then there is nothing that can be done."

"Drom, if one recognizes the absence of doing, this is perfect equanimity."

"Though this may be true, does it help at all?"

"Drom, it is not that it does not help. There is no doer."

"Master, isn't this because there is nothing to do?"

"Now you have understood, Drom."

"So how should one practice the immeasurable thoughts?"

"Drom, forcefully and carefully, practice all four."

"Won't excitation and laxity occur?"

"Drom, one therefore practices all four of them."

"Aren't all four more powerful than just one?"

"Drom, yet one is the antidote of the other."

"Won't all four cancel each other out?"

"Drom, what reasons do you have?"

"What happens when clay pots attack each other?"

"Drom, what are you saying? How can it be similar to that?"

"Though they may not be similar, still there will be a fault."

"Drom, the head of laxity is kept down by excitation."

"Won't excitation alone arise then?"

"Drom, the head of excitation is in turn kept down by laxity."

"In that case, won't one be kept busy with these two?"

"No, Drom; rather, one balances the two."

"What happens when they are in equilibrium?"

"Drom, it is like the absence of illness that occurs when the four elements are in equilibrium."

"Can't one meditate on just any one?"

"Drom, practice what you can."

"I am afraid that excitation and laxity might occur."

"Drom, have less doubt about this."

"Should one meditate when they do not occur?"

"Drom, one can meditate again and again."

"But if one sinks into laxity, can this still become a path?"

"Drom, can one meditate while mental laxity is most pronounced?"

"This will not bring existence to an end, Master."

"Drom, I also maintain the same."

"So how does one lay the defects of laxity to rest?"

"Drom, when the faults of laxity are recognized it will be dispelled."

"Master, today's conversation has soothed my mind."

"Drom, I have never indulged in mere meaningless chatter."

"Master, there is, therefore, a collection on dispelling mental laxity."

"Drom, there is a collection on dispelling both laxity and excitation."

"So, though there are many teachings, there are three collections.

"Even though there have been numerous conversations, with my queries and your responses, if you summarize them, it is simply this:

Since you take no pleasure in negative deeds,
when a thought of self-importance arises,
at that instant deflate your pride
and recall your teacher's instructions.

When discouraged thoughts arise,
uplift your mind and meditate on the emptiness of both.[94]

"There is nothing other than this."

This concludes the fourteenth chapter of the *Jewel Garland of Dialogues*, "Meditating on Perfect Equanimity of Excitation and Mental Laxity through Cutting the Root of Suffering."

8. The Two Examinations

ONCE AGAIN, at that perfect site and in the presence of the sublime teacher, our teacher [Dromtönpa], the perfect spiritual guide and yogi of hidden conduct, made the following plea: "Sublime teacher, pray listen. This treatise encompassing such vast themes is extremely difficult. So please teach us, now, a profound practice that summarizes all the points."

Thus, Atiśa responded:

Excessive speech is a cause for nonvirtue;
excessive distraction is a cause for nonvirtue;
words of praise and words of disparagement,
pleasant utterances and unpleasant ones,

Distorted speech and truthful speech,
explicit statements and implicit statements,
praise through insult and disparagement through praise,
hurtful speech and arrogant speech,

Voicing senseless speech on account of affliction,
speech of attachment and speech of aversion,
deluded speech and speech of envy,
conceited speech and speech of untamed views,

Lies that deceive and humorous lies,
words wishing to mock others, both wise and foolish,

ordinary words aimed at destroying important people,
"kill," "hit," and words that seek to humiliate,

Words of superficial friendliness, flattery, and conceit,
words of deals and aspirations,
words of battle and of masculine pride—
even the slightest of these gives rise to strong affliction.

Sentient beings are born with affliction as the cause.
Because envy and aversion are inborn,
when one person is praised another is angered.
Through needless anger, virtuous roots are destroyed.

Using foul names they evince bitterness.
With a praise for one, one hundred are insulted.
Through the faults of speech, one attracts enemies;
through the faults of speech, one loses friends.

Through the faults of speech, I have heard,
ploughshares run one thousand times over one's tongue!
Even when pleasant words are abundant,
distinctions are made through differences in tone!

When you praise someone only a little,
it strikes at his weakness and creates suspicion.
Praise can turn someone into an enemy.
If an undeserving person is praised,
he will well up with anger even more.
If someone worthy of praise is spoken to in measured words,
he becomes angry, as if you have insulted him.

In general if there are many it's hard to speak;
harder still is it to speak to those not kindred in mind;

harder still is it to speak to those who are ambitious;
harder still is it to speak to those who are small minded.

The end of a jest becomes a quarrel;
the end of such speech is conflict between two bodies;
the end of the body is loss of life;
the end of life is a journey to lower realms.

This concludes the first examination pertaining to speech.
Foolishness is not to abandon these despite knowing this.

As for the second examination, analyze the speech.
With respect to the analysis, first probe the objects.
If they are many, silence is best;
if they are faithful ones, speak of goodness;
if they are learned people, praise their higher qualities;
if they are disciplined ones, praise their discipline;
if they are kindhearted ones, speak of the practices;
if they are evil-ridden beings, gently avoid them;
if it serves as a remedy, then speak of anything;
otherwise, refrain from the fault of speech.

Second, when you speak to others,
bring the voice to your throat [and observe],
is there an expectation or not?
Is it laden with afflictions, like attachment and aversion,
    or not?

Is there attachment borne of selfish desire or not?
Is there animosity toward others or not?
Do the words become defamation or not?
Is it senseless speech or lying words?

Is it divisive speech or harsh words?
Will it hurt through insinuation or confrontation?
Will it hurt directly or indirectly?
Is it the word of a noble one or of a childish person?
Is it meaningful or not meaningful?
If yes, send it to the mouth's entrance;
if not, dissolve it into the *aḥ* at your throat.

Furthermore, when in the presence of one who is absorbed
    in meditation,
do not engage in recitation;
In the presence of a hardened Dharma defamer,
do not engage in recitation and practice.

Moreover, proclaiming the Great Vehicle
to a Lesser Vehicle practitioner constitutes a fault.
Though your devotion to your teachers,
preceptors, masters, and so on might be strong, do not
    speak their praises
in front of those who are laden with prejudice.

Proclaiming what is secret to unsuitable ordinary people
is a great harbinger of ill effects indeed;
in brief, until you attain superior knowledge,
it is vital to guard your speech in all its forms.

In particular, be decisive when in the midst of many.
Those who have turned their backs to the Dharma,
the haughty—eloquent in oration and abundant in speech—
they judge all: the high, middle, and low.

When some are praised, others become upset;
by speaking for the benefit of the collective, individuals
    are upset.

When concerns of individuals are raised, the collective rises
    as an enemy;
when there is nothing to say, meaningless gibberish is spoken.
One hundred respond to one, one thousand respond to the
    hundred!
In the end, words destroy your roots of virtue;
the haughty man arrives in the hells!

Blessed by the māra of distraction,
amid many one speaks unceasing chatter.
Though everyone gathered is seething,
resorting to laughter, one seduces them with praise.
Strike the unruly tongue with a whip.

So Drom Jé, analyze your speech;
Cease inferior speech and endeavor in mantra recitation.
Though you may hear pleasant or hostile words,
remain like a mute person.

If even pratyekabuddhas guard their speech,
why wouldn't the excellent bodhisattvas do so?
If you instruct at the right time, this is wise;
if your words hit their mark, this is heroic.

If words are excellent, they are sublime Dharma;
if they turn into poetry, they will grab the senses;
if you understand, you'll pay heed to all your speech;
it is vital, therefore, to constantly examine your speech.

This concludes the second, the collection on examining
objects and speech, so analyze this.

"Atiśa, most excellent in speech:
Not sullied by defects of speech,

you are proficient in speech, the glory of beings.
Excellent speaker of Dharma, pray listen.

"This is advice for life among the multitude.
Now I request a teaching to practice when alone,
the most essential point that encompasses everything,
a teaching for those living in solitude."

"Drom, when alone probe your mind."
    "It will be clearer if this is unraveled by means of a teacher's method."
    "Drom, without mind who would grasp at objects?"
    "As there is no grasper they would not be grasped at."
    "Drom, with no mind who would speak to whom?"
    "As there would be no speaker, why be attached and averse?"
    "Drom, such is the nature of subjects and objects."
    "What is the foundation and root of the mind?"
    "Drom, I haven't found that reality."
    "How is it that you have not found this?"
    "Drom, because there is no arising, abiding, or ceasing."
    "How is it that we perceive diversity?"
    "Drom, it is absence of appearance appearing."
    "Is not appearance thatness?"
    "Drom, what is it that is called *appearance*?"
    "It is the perception of diverse objects."
    "Drom, is it the object that is perceived or is it the mind itself?"
    "It is the mind that perceives objects."
    "Drom, now the time has come to analyze that mind."
    "The time has come for the mode of such analysis."
    "Drom, show me your preceding awareness."
    "What is past cannot be shown here."
    "Drom, then show me your future awareness."

"Can the future be here now?"

"Drom, in that case show me your present awareness."

"There is nothing to point my finger at."

"Drom, why is that so?"

"That is what I am asking *you*."

"Drom, even all the buddhas come to a halt on this point."

"Aren't they versed in everything?"

"Drom, it cannot be that the learned have understood falsely."

"In that case does the mind itself not exist?"

"Drom, they know it as if it exists."

"Who, then, wanders in this realm of cyclic existence?"

"Drom, the 'clever,' essenceless ones wander there."

"Are we not all like this?"

"Drom, you too are like a stuffed dummy."

"We grasp at an essence where there is none."

"Drom, this is the behavior of samsaric beings."

"Is it not the case that behavior does not exist?"

"Drom, who is claiming that behavior exists?"

"You just spoke of behavior."

"Drom, trust not in the truth of conventional words."

"In that case were you being a liar?"

"Drom, there is no need for being one, for things are naturally so."

"Can lies become the path?"

"Drom, everything is said to be illusion-like."

"Is the mind, too, an illusory mind?"

"Drom, it is a dream, an apparition, a mere luminosity."

"How can one do the generation and completion stages within a mere luminosity?"

"Drom, construct all the mandalas within."

"How does one construct a mandala?"

"Drom, as mere luminosity, as mere awareness, and as mere purity."

"What is the significance of doing such?"

"Drom, so that no disclosure of secrets will occur and realization will increase."

"Won't there be obstacles to this?"

"Drom, undetected by Māra, one will become fully awakened."

"Should one practice method after emptiness?"

"Drom, all method and wisdom will increase within."

"What is such a person called?"

"Drom, 'upholder of hidden yogic conduct.'"

"Please wrap all this up."

"Drom, let go with ease the generated love and compassion, which are luminous."

"How should one examine the mind when attracted to a form?"

"Drom, examine the shape and color of that mind."

"How should one examine it when attracted to a sound?"

"Drom, examine whether the mind has a sound."

"How should one examine it when attracted to a smell?"

"Drom, examine whether the mind has a smell."

"How should one examine it when attracted to a taste?"

"Drom, examine whether the mind has a taste."

"How should one examine it when attracted to tactile sensations?"

"Drom, examine its texture."

"How should one examine it when attracted to phenomena?"

"Drom, apart from these sense objects, what reality-itself is there?"

"Master, there are fabrications of conceptualization."

"Drom, examine concepts, too, in the same manner."

"How should one examine the examiner itself?"

"Drom, when the body disintegrates where will the limbs be?"

"They arise invariably in relation to the body."

"Drom, it is vital to constantly examine in this manner."

"What should one do when, following such examination, everything is dismantled?"

"Drom, unable to find anything, they will vanish into space like a rainbow."

"Is this nonfinding most excellent?"

"Drom, finding and not finding differentiates an ordinary person from a noble one."

"What if, with repeated searching, nothing is found?"

"Drom, one repeatedly sees one's own standpoint."

"Should one place one's mind on this nonfinding?"

"Drom, if one releases it with ease this is sublime."

"What is the lineage of this essential point?"

"Drom, it is the Conqueror, Tārā, and myself."

"How should I share this with others?"

"Drom, accept those who are suitable vessels into your heart drop."

"Does this accord with the mandala referred to earlier?"

"Drom, the mandala of the mind is more important."

"What are the favorable conditions for this practice?"

"Drom, elaborately perform the seven limbs."

"These two examinations are most beneficial indeed."

"Drom, understand them and put them into practice."

"Master, though your responses to my queries were numerous,
when summarized, there are the seven riches;
if further condensed, there are the two examinations.
You have revealed these two examinations in a full chapter.
If the two examinations are summed up, they are this:

Among others guard your speech;
when alone guard your mind.[95]

"On this auspicious point all points converge.
This is the jewel garland of well-spoken insights!
This is the conduct concealing the sacred seal!"

❦

Your crown adorned by Amitābha, the conqueror,[96]
in whom all jewels of benefit and happiness are stacked,
O lord, we touch our heads to your feet.

Through such an amiable dialogue,
may all be amiable and flourish.
There is no doubt that this root-like summary
is the teacher's own word.

Though compiled separately, no name was given;
clearly it is a dialogue on the *Jewel Garland*.
Also, the queries and answers were not stated there.
Embracing these words of Master Atiśa,
instantly they were transcribed in letters;
the letters were in the Bodhgaya style.

Homage to the sacred teaching of Avalokiteśvara!
May it flourish in all corners not yet perceived;
may oath-breaking and moral degeneration cease;
may all latent propensities be destroyed;
may we depart from the land of ignorance;
may we traverse the levels and paths in sequence;
may there be no obstacles on the path;
may we become omniscient for the benefit of all;
may the Kadam flourish to the farthest corners;
may it remain lotus-like on a lotus;
may it always be with the learned, the disciplined,
    and the kind;
may I become a lord of all beings without exception;
may I enjoy the mine of dual accumulations;
may all be led to this inexhaustible mine;

may the stream of this river that sustains
the lineage of the Three Jewels always remain.

This concludes the twenty-third chapter of the *Jewel Garland of Dialogues*, "The Two Examinations."

THE SON TEACHINGS

THE FINAL TEXT in our volume is a selection from the Son Teachings, the second volume of the *Book of Kadam*. More specifically, it is the penultimate chapter, namely chapter 22 of that collection. As noted earlier, unlike the Father Teachings, the Son Teachings is essentially a collection of birth stories of Dromtön-pa's former lives, twenty-two in all. The twenty-third chapter is an assortment of miscellaneous passages: proclamations of auspiciousness, prophesies, a song on the view of ultimate reality, and others. Of the birth stories, the first twenty were narrated at the request of Ngok Lekpai Sherap and the final two were told in response to queries from Khutön Tsöndrü Yungdrung. What binds this collection of Drom's birth stories to the Father Teachings is that, like the Father Teachings, (1) these birth stories were revealed by Master Atiśa; (2) they are part of the spiritual teachings given during the three-year sojourn at the retreat of Yerpa; (3) they are all grounded in or spring from discussion of specific lines from Atiśa's *Bodhisattva's Jewel Garland*; and finally, (4) these teachings are intimately connected with the person of Dromtönpa.

The Tibetan text of the Son Teachings opens with a prologue that sets the context of these teachings. We read:

> When Atiśa and his son were residing in Yerpa on the crest of Mount Lhari Nyingpo, Ngok Lekpai Sherap made the following plea to Drom Gyalwai

Jungné: "For three years you, the conqueror and son, have taught the most profound and inconceivable teaching. This uncommon and unique teaching in twenty-three chapters is called the *Jewel Garland of Dialogues*. In it you state, 'Discard all lingering doubts / and strive with dedication in your practice.' So how did you discard all lingering doubts and strive in meditative practice in the past? Pray, with an affectionate heart, do tell me."[97]

In response, Drom, with characteristic humility, states that since he is an ordinary person chained by many fetters like the rest, he could not have relinquished all the doubts in the past. He admits, however, that for those who seek liberation, it is generally necessary to discard all lingering doubts. This then leads Ngok to turn to Master Atiśa with the following appeal:

This Gyalwai Jungné conceals all his higher qualities and does not reveal them, so please, teacher, speak to us about how his qualities came to be. He does have higher qualities, and you, the teacher, do not resort to exaggeration or denigration. By hearing his qualities we will cultivate faith and reverence. This could also benefit future sentient beings as well. So teacher, please do reveal Drom's higher qualities to us.

To this, Master Atiśa replies that Drom's qualities, in their entirety, resemble a treasury of precious jewels, some of which would lie beyond the comprehension of ordinary people. He then counsels Ngok not to speak of these qualities to others and reminds him that what he is going to teach is essentially for Ngok's own retention. However, before Atiśa can launch into enumerating Drom's qualities, Drom voices his objection by exclaiming that there are so many profound teachings that could be taught, teachings that are beneficial through all stages of practice—beginning, middle, and end. "So what point is there," he asks, "in recounting the various ways in which Drom wandered in the cycle of existence?"

Ngok responds to Drom's protestation with the powerful appeal: "O spiritual mentor, I am not someone with a large mouth and a small brain. Leaving five hundred monks behind, I have come here to sever the ropes of my lingering doubts; so even if you won't tell us, please do not prevent Atiśa from teaching us. Look at my head and my wrinkles as well, and sustain me with your heart. Pray, sustain me with your heart."

Atiśa, moved by Ngok's appeal, responds: "Lekpai Sherap, you are right. I have decided to speak. Yet, since this is a heart counsel for the three of us—father and sons—alone, do not spread it to others." Opening with the advice that this particular set of teachings be kept discreet, Atiśa commences the first story with the line, "In the town of Kapila, there once lived. . . ."

9. The Spiritual Mentor's Birth as Prince Śaraṇadatta

ON ANOTHER OCCASION when the conqueror Atiśa, his son Gyalwai Jungné, and Lekpai Sherap of Sangphu were residing upon Tārā's right knee,[98] Khutön Tsöndrü Yungdrung came before them and, just as before, having made all the offerings such as the silver mandala, asked Atiśa: "Just as it appears in the remaining part of the *Jewel Garland of Dialogues*, I ask you to tell us, as you mentioned yesterday, the story of our spiritual mentor's past birth that could lead to great laughter."

Atiśa replied, "Shall I tell the one about a sharp beak, or about his birth as someone kind, most kind? Or shall I tell one that can withstand the test of time?"

"How many births were there when he was kind, most kind?" inquired Khutön.

Atiśa replied, "Many times he was learned, many times he was disciplined, later he was many times born kind, and many times he was born as a great king. As for all the other life stories, even the Buddha would be unable to count them."

The spiritual mentor interjected, "Tell the story of how I once dug up an elephant's corpse." Atiśa agreed and told the following story:

"Once, in the past, in a town called Sukhāvatī, the great Drom was born as a religious king named Śaraṇadatta. You, great Khu, were born as his minister Samudācāra, and my great Amé[99] was born as the queen Asaṅgakoṣa. She was devout in venerating the high Three Jewels, compassionate in caring for lowly, ill-mannered beings, and for those in between, she donned the garments of shame and conscience. She cared for everyone as if they were her children.

"At the center of this town was a well, extremely wide and deep. One day an elephant fell in the well, and despite their efforts, no one could rescue the elephant. As its body lay there, decomposed and rotten, all the nāgas, who were so concerned with cleanliness, ran away, and so the well dried up. As everyone in town suffered from lack of water, it occurred to King Śaraṇadatta, 'The townspeople are suffering from lack of water. With the power of the blessed buddhas, who are endowed with great compassion, I will extract the elephant's carcass and lead all these beings to happiness.' Thus both the king and his minister went to the well, where the king commanded his minister, 'Look after my body so that no harm comes to it. I will enter the elephant's carcass with my consciousness and bring it out.'

"Issuing this command, he went to the bottom of the well. The minister, however, left his own body, entered the king's body, and maimed his own body with lacerations. After the king had entered the elephant's body and brought it out of the well, he noticed that his own body was now gone and only the maimed body of his minister was left behind. Seeing he could not enter the minister's body, he spotted a parrot's corpse with no injuries and entered it.

"At that time a large number of merchants were congregating in a nearby garden. At night the parrot would help round up the caravan animals that had gone astray. He would sing comforting lullabies and give solace to the merchants by encouraging them to sleep with peace. He would sing wondrous songs like the following:

Human life is so difficult to find.
With sun-like faculties free of darkness,
you now pursue your mundane aspirations,

but on the day you die,
all the possessions you acquired with such effort will be
    left behind.
If you journey alone and naked,
seek the lasting garment of morality;
think that nothing else is meaningful.

When self-grasping attachment enters your heart,
you'll deceive even your father, who deserves your respect.
'Though one [father] may look after many [children],
the many cannot carry the weight of the one';
unreliable, false thoughts increase in them toward their
    kind one.

You have failed to see karma and its long-term effects.
Even if you engage in minor virtues
that grant some partial joys,
if you fail to prevent subtle obstacles,
you'll say, 'Dharma is not true either, for such things occur.'
With no means of escape, you'll go to the lower realms.

Alas! All you merchants who have gathered here,
one day death will definitely come;
do something profitable so that you'll be happy then.
Even though you continue to aspire to have them,
wealth and possessions only increase your pain.

The pain of searching for what you do not have
and the pain of guarding what you do have—
you have harbored these over one hundred lifetimes.
Listen, O most eager merchants,
beneath each possession is an enemy;
each enemy brings a suffering,
all of which are then hung around the owner's neck.

If you fall prey to thirst for pleasure and wealth,
you will experience a great mass of suffering in return.
Recognize this and put it into practice.

"The merchants felt deep satisfaction, and the chief merchant adopted the parrot. One day the parrot flew over his old palace and observed what had happened there. He saw that his minister had assumed his own body. His queen also looked sad and was given to sighing; the palace and the servants within it had lost their luster. Even the auspicious music was nowhere to be heard, so the parrot inquired:

In the past the king, queen, and their retinue
lived in harmony and enjoyed wealth and spirituality;
the palace was filled with joyful music.
These days, however, even you, the queen, look dejected.
The king also appears to be a coward.
O queen, be at peace and speak to me.

"Hearing the parrot speak, the queen felt some peace and replied:

O learned bird, listen to me.
Though such prosperity existed here in the past,
today, a demonic force has robbed us of our joys;
into the depths of the well from which countless drank
a careless elephant had fallen,
so the well dried up, placing all of us in misery.

Unable to bear this the king went to extract it.
Although his minister accompanied him in order to assist,
he did not return; the lord alone returned.
Unlike before, he has become sharp-tongued.
Even the kingdom has lost its majesty;

without musicians, song and dance are no more.
No objects worthy of veneration have appeared since then.
It must have been due to the minister's good fortune that
    we had these in the past;
now that the minister is no more, perhaps they, too, are lost.
Unless, of course, the king suffered a tragedy;
do you know anything about this, O learned bird?

"In response, the parrot spoke:

Listen well, Asaṅgakoṣa.
I am King Śaraṇadatta.
When, out of concern for beings,
I was extracting the elephant from the well,
I entrusted my body to my companion Samudācāra,
and my consciousness went to the bottom of the well
and entered the elephant's corpse.
When I returned to the surface, the minister's body lay
    injured,
and the king's body was nowhere to be found.

Seeing no point in entering the minister's body,
I entered this body that I found.
For days I have been living in the garden
amid the transiently gathered merchants;
I have sincerely taught them the Dharma and made
    them happy.
Today, when I returned here and saw you,
though joyful, I felt unhappy and was saddened.

Go to the merchant today.
Buy me and joyfully bring me home.
Then, when the king is having his meal,
I will lie in a pile of earth, and as I get up,

I will flap my wings and fill his meal with dirt.
He will then beat me and I will die.

Then cry aloud, 'My parrot!
Tell me a beautiful story!
Flap your wings about with joy!'
Uttering such words, you should weep.
Then the king will say, 'Don't cry. I will revive the parrot!'
Leaving his body in the palace, he will enter
the parrot's body and speak to you,
and as you respond with expressions of joy,
I will then enter the king's body.

"The instant the queen heard this, she was delighted.
Immediately she went to the merchant and asked,
'Please sell me your bird.'
The merchant refused to comply.
'No, I won't sell. I need it myself,' he replied.
In response, the parrot said:

Please do sell me to this queen.
For if the winged creature escapes into the sky,
it will be of no value and you will lose the merchandise
itself.
Now I will set the price for my own self;
O queen, trade three animals for me:
one riding horse and two buffaloes.

"Having traded in this way, she returned to the palace.
The parrot spoke in metrical verses,
and the queen responded with joy.
One day, as the parrot executed what they had planned before,
the king hit the parrot with a club and killed him.
Then, as the queen reacted in the ways described before,

the king, saying, 'Don't cry. I will revive the parrot,'
went inside its body and revived the parrot.

"As he spoke and flew around,
the king then entered his own body.
The palace interior became filled with light;
the entire palace became most radiant.
As if by the shining of the sun, people felt their minds
    refreshed.
Then the king revealed his hidden treasures.
Showing them to the bird, he declared:

By deceiving the one who had rendered you kindness,
O minister, you have now become an animal.
Had you not violated your own body,
I would have worn the minister's armor;
I would have rendered you my service;
yet with a distorted mind, you destroyed your own body.
With no better body, I became a bird;
with a king-like body, you failed to rule.
Without merit, the body is of no use.
I have no need for the kingdom myself,
but since you cannot sustain the land,
I will assume my own body and work for others.
Be happy, O lady Asaṅga.
Gather merit, you who are forceful in giving;
nurture well those in your circle, O most sincere one.

Birth in the higher realms is a royal palace;
you've found the excellent island of a precious human life,
so in this ship sailing across to the other shore,
without being trapped by the tides that press down
on the ocean of birth, aging, sickness, and death,
travel in peace and with happiness.

"As such sounds of the Dharma echoed,
the queen's thoughts were filled with Dharma,
and on the basis of firm one-pointed meditation,
she placed her mind, without wavering, on the ultimate mode.

"In a subsequent experience of clear awareness,
she saw, in the future, an emanation of a sugata
taming countless beings in a central land and in the
    hinterlands.
She saw that at that time there would be countless yogis with
    excellent qualities
all aspiring for awakening.
Having found the supreme hidden conduct,
[the sugata] would thoroughly suppress the tides of the
    hinterlands.

> May I be not separated from this sugata emanation,
> traveling across India and Tibet.
> May I bow at your feet, O Dharma king,
> and venerate you in the ultimate expanse of reality.

> Again, in front of the seven Mount Merus,
> inside the glorious royal palace,
> where the scriptures radiate with brilliance,
> may I meditate upon the ultimate nature
> on a turquoise lake with one thousand swirling spokes
> in the presence of numerous golden lotus trees.

> May the minister with a parrot's body
> transform his misdeeds as well, and,
> even if he becomes a learned one among the learned,
> may he bow at your feet[100]
> and spread Dharma wealth and auspiciousness.

[The minister:] Listen to me, O emanation master,
by bowing at your feet
how will I become a learned one among the learned?

"The master then replied:

In the future, about twenty generations from now,
many will bow at my feet.
Twenty most learned ones will emerge in succession,
learned in various fields of knowledge.
In the end, too, just as you have prayed,
I will tame you in the hinterlands
and venerate the sugata emanation;
and may we then depart to the place of goodness.
May your aspirations be fulfilled just as you wish.

"Ah, out of compassion, the sovereign
created an attractive body with magical eyes,
clad in most attractive garments,
and made the minister's consciousness enter it.
At mealtimes he reverted into a parrot.
He applied himself to spiritual activities;
with remorseful heart he purified his misdeeds.
With resolve he venerated others with devotion.

"One day an undamaged corpse
of a youthful brahman man was found.
The sovereign washed it with perfumed water
and summoned the minister's consciousness into it.
He taught him the various well-spoken insights.
Thus, among those who were learned,
he excelled in linguistics, logic, and the arts.
Then he trained him in apparent phenomena,
insubstantial, resembling magical and optical illusions.

In composition and exposition of eloquent works,
thus did he attain the status of a supreme scholar.
He also became skilled in healing the sick.

"Then an emanation monk appeared
in the space above the king and spoke to Samudācāra:

> O brahman youth, become a renunciate.
> Place yourself in the solitude of forests;
> discipline your mind, and in all your lives
> we two shall care for you.

"Then the emanation monk conferred the vows upon him;
the minister, having prepared his provisions,
lived a satisfying life in the forest.
Asaṅgakoṣa vanished into space;
Śaraṇadatta's pursuit of beings' welfare was uninterrupted.
Never discouraged, his forbearance was great;
having led many beings to Dharma,
attachment free, he departed to the ultimate expanse.

"O great Khu, your end was excellent. This was also the auspicious condition that allowed us both to sustain you. Given these reasons, one who is known as Gyalwai Jungné is indeed endowed with the inconceivable qualities of enlightened deeds and activities. Since you two—Khu and Ngok—have asked for it, I have given you the full narration of this list of stories without omission on how, with no sense of despair, Dromtönpa worked for others' welfare on numerous occasions. As explained before, after Gyalwai Jungné, many ordained renunciates will appear. They will bow at his feet and revere him, and they will make aspiration prayers for the future. Although I could say a lot of things, such as how they are all his own emanations, how they are directly blessed by that deity, what specific individuals they will become in the future, and what shall be their names and so on, Drom has repeatedly sealed me from speaking about these.

"Nevertheless, since it is possible that, within the minds of the spiritual trainees of special fortune, naturally arising letters can appear, a book could appear. However, given that it is difficult for those who follow the path by means of faith to uphold the book, read it, reveal it extensively to others, comprehend it within their minds in its entirety, or sustain it with perfection, it is not in the form of conventional letters. Even if it were, there would be inconsistent editions. Therefore, to help you ascertain the stories, and on the basis of drawing from various beneficial activities, I have given you here a very rough outline that you can fathom. Now, do not preach this in places where people lack faith and are heedless. Do not teach this to ordinary beings who do not share the same spiritual tradition. This then is my seal."

Atiśa continued, "Again, those who have faith in Kadam, those who practice Kadam, whose minds can contain it, who have conviction in it, who practice it as their heart drop, and who have deep admiration for their teacher's higher qualities should explain this. Moreover, there are those who, despite having respect for the teacher, view him as an ordinary upāsaka; those who make judgments about greater and lesser teachers; those who think in terms of such judgments as, 'He has this much knowledge,' 'His name is this,' 'He was born at such a place,' 'He performed such activities,' or 'He relied upon six teachers and then passed away'; and those who assert, 'Such and such a person committed evil karma.' As for these many people, who while having respect [for their teacher], grasp at limited judgments, you should definitely teach them this book by showing them what constitutes the tradition of Kadam.

"Again, there could be regions where the following occurs: masters are conceited on account of their status; the greedy are conceited on account of their wealth; the powerful are conceited on account of their authority; the civilized are conceited on account of their breeding; the haughty are conceited on account of their strength; or the youth are conceited on account of their beauty. You should not teach this book to such conceited ones.

"Why? Because they do not value the source of precious jewels as such but treat it as a heap of rubbish. Furthermore, even if you are a sublime being, if all do not recognize you as valid, your teaching may not be recognized as perfect because of [lack of esteem for] you. You risk having your teaching derided.

"As for the teacher, he should be like this: he should be a spiritual mentor revered by all, a bodhisattva who is respectful toward all beings, and a person who is held as authoritative by others. On the part of the individual himself, he should neither exaggerate nor denigrate but should examine the suitability of the vessels just as explained in the book. Such a person should teach the book.

"Furthermore, if there is an opportunity to turn a person with wrong views away from such views, you should teach this. If there is an opportunity to enhance virtues such as faith, you should teach this. If you have the text, visualize the text as the spiritual mentor and, imagining yourself as Avalokiteśvara, recite the words of the *Jewel Garland.* If you have no text, seek apology [for possible omissions and errors], but teach the book nonetheless."

After Atiśa had spoken, Lotsāwa[101] commented: "In a certain part of India, a paṇḍita once had to climb a staircase thirteen times, and so on . . .[102] Once, when Nāgārjuna and King Dechö Sangpo were alchemically producing gold on the basis of a corpse,[103] the king went to Śativana cemetery between thirteen and twenty-one times to try and bring back a corpse. The master commanded, 'Until you have brought me the corpse, do not look back, do not speak, and do not rest, for if you do any of these you will fail to bring back the corpse.' However, because the corpse told stories like these [ones I've mentioned (e.g., the paṇḍita and the stairs)], the king would fail in his mindfulness and exclaim, 'What a wonderful story!' Saying, 'You cannot keep secret what is meant to be kept secret,' the corpse would then be lost and would not be retained.

"This corpse also told a story about two birds. Finally, the corpse asked, 'On each of the thirteen steps on a staircase, there are thirteen birds, and in each of the bird's beaks there are thirteen grains of barley. How many grains are there?' Before he could complete the calculation, the king reached the master's presence. Then, three nights later, they applied alchemy to the zombie, which is said to still exist in India, transforming it into gold. I heard all of these stories most clearly from an Indian paṇḍita. He would count the golden hills to be between thirteen and twenty-one."

Atiśa observed, "This translator has heard all sorts of things! Keep in your mind this story of how, failing to heed his master's command, the king lost the corpse so many times, and seal your mouth tight. Secrecy is important.

"In closing, Khu, irrespective of where he took birth, this Drom never defamed the Dharma, he admired whatever teachings he found most affinity with, he strove both day and night in pursuit of the ten spiritual activities, he dedicated the virtues of the three times for the benefit of all sentient beings, he was never divorced from the seven limbs, and recognizing defective forms of speech, he ensured that he was free from the faults of mind."

Thus, from the presentation of the lives of Drom Gyalwai Jungné, which have been made complete to Khu, this concludes the twenty-second life cycle, the chapter on how our spiritual mentor took birth as King Śaraṇadatta, which is based upon the following lines:

> Never defame the teachings.
> In whatever practices you admire,

with aspiration and the ten spiritual deeds,
strive diligently, dividing day and night.

Whatever virtues you gather through the three times,
dedicate them toward unexcelled great awakening.
Distribute your merit to all sentient beings
and utter the peerless aspiration prayers
of the seven limbs at all times.

If you proceed thus, you'll swiftly perfect merit and wisdom
and eliminate the two defilements.
Since your human existence will be meaningful,
you'll attain unexcelled enlightenment.

The wealth of faith, the wealth of morality,
the wealth of giving, the wealth of learning,
the wealth of conscience, the wealth of shame,
and the wealth of insight—these are the seven riches.

These precious and excellent jewels
are the seven inexhaustible riches.
Do not speak of these to those not human.
Among others guard your speech;
when alone guard your mind.[104]

With these, the two teachings for Khutön from among the
twenty-two Son Teachings are complete.

Notes

1. Cited in Yeshe Döndrup's *Treasury of Gems*, p. 230. On Gönpawa, see pp. 47–48 below.
2. A saying of the master Tsangpa Gyaré as cited in Chenga Lodrö Gyaltsen's *Initial Mind Training*, p. 27a5.
3. Cited in Yeshé Döndrup's *Treasury of Gems*, p. 237.
4. Cited in Lechen Kunga Gyaltsen's *Lamp Illuminating the History of the Kadam Tradition*, p. 226.
5. Cited in Chenga Lodrö Gyaltsen's *Initial Mind Training*, p. 16a6.
6. Some sections of this essay as well as my short introduction to part II of the book, on the *Book of Kadam* and its spiritual legacy, have been adapted from my introduction in *The Book of Kadam: The Core Texts*, which appeared as volume 2 of *The Library of Tibetan Classics*.
7. Hubert Decleer makes this comparison in his paper "Master Atiśa in Nepal: The Tham Bahīl and Five Stūpas according to the *'Brom ston Itinerary*," p. 43. For a succinct account in English of Atiśa's life in general and the Ngari rulers' efforts in bringing Atiśa to Tibet, see Pabongka Rinpoche, *Liberation in the Palm of Your Hand*, pp. 28–58, and Alaka Chattopadhyaya's *Atiśa and Tibet*, pp. 291–306.
8. Lechen, *Lamp Illuminating the History of the Kadam Tradition*, pp. 5–6.
9. Gö Lotsāwa Shönu Pal, *Blue Annals*, vol. I, p. 395. An alternative rendering of the passage appears on page 326 of Roerich's translation.
10. Khutön Tsöndrü Yungdrung (1011–75), Ngok Lekpai Sherap (eleventh century), the founder of the scholastic monastery

Sangphu, and Dromtönpa, whose personal name is Gyalwai Jungné (1004–64).

11. *Four Hundred Stanzas on the Middle Way*, 8:5, 9a7.

12. This is a reference to the three key elements of an action: namely, the object of the action, the agent of the act, and the act itself, which together form the basis of grasping at the substantial reality of actions and events.

13. This is the Tibetan ruler who, together with his uncle Yeshé Ö, was instrumental in bringing Atiśa to Tibet. It was, in fact, at the behest of Jangchup Ö, as attested by the opening lines in the text itself, that Atiśa composed the famous *Lamp for the Path to Enlightenment*.

14. Mara refers to an obstructive force, often personified in the classical Buddhist sources, that leads sentient beings astray toward the path of nonvirtue, harm, and immorality.

15. Known also as Shangtsün of Yerpa, he was a student of Atiśa and later took teachings from the three Kadam brothers as well. In accordance with Atiśa's instruction, Shangtsün dedicated his entire life to meditative practice and was believed to have experientially realized the truth of impermanence. For a brief biographical note on Yerpa, see page 49 of this volume.

16. The four pursuits are farming, trade, finance, and raising livestock.

17. "Laying bare the bones of your heart" is a vernacular Tibetan expression for making strenuous effort.

18. On these disciples, see the biographical sketches that precede their sayings below. For more on Dromtönpa, see part II below on the *Book of Kadam*.

19. This is the first of the four stages of the path of preparation, the other three being "peak," "forbearance," and "supreme Dharma."

20. See note 12 above.

21. Śāntideva, *Guide to the Bodhisattva's Way of Life*, 8:129–30.

22. This short biography of Gönpawa is drawn from Lechen Künga Gyaltsen's *Lamp Illuminating the History of the Kadam Tradition*, pp. 212–20.

23. A brief biography of Yerpa Shangtsün exists in Lechen's *Lamp Illuminating the History of the Kadam Tradition*, pp. 157–59, and

a selection of Yerpa's teachings can be found in Yeshé Döndrup's *Treasury of Gems*, pp. 133–34.

24. An English translation of the *Blue Compendium*, literally the *Blue Udder*, will be available in *Stages of the Buddha's Teaching: Three Selected Texts*, volume 10 of *The Library of Tibetan Classics*.

25. A succinct biography of Potowa can be found in Lechen's *Lamp Illuminating the History of the Kadam Tradition*, pp. 215b4–224a1.

26. For a woman practitioner, the object of this meditation would typically be that of a man's body, the key point being that one should take whatever happens to be the object of one's sexual attachment as the focus of foulness meditation.

27. Buddhaghoṣa's *Visuddhimagga* gives a list of ten aspects of foulness meditation, which are, in addition to the seven mentioned here: (1) scattered, (2) hacked and scattered, and (3) bleeding. The order of the visualization of these aspects presented in Buddhaghoṣa's text is slightly different from the one presented here. See *Path of Purification*, chap. VI, pp. 179–90.

28. As before, if the practitioner is a nun, she would typically relate this meditation to a man.

29. A succinct biography of Chengawa can be found in Lechen's *Lamp Illuminating the History of the Kadam Tradition*, pp. 164b1–68b3.

30. Śāntideva, *Guide to the Bodhisattva's Way of Life*, 6:106.

31. Ibid., 6:42.

32. Ibid., 6:37–38.

33. These four lines can be found in Śāntideva's *Guide to the Bodhisattva's Way of Life*, 9:151 and 152, where the first two lines and the last are part of verse 151, while line three is part of verse 152. It is conceivable that Chengawa is citing from a slightly different redaction of the Tibetan text of *Guide to the Bodhisattva's Way of Life*. For a discussion of the various redactions of Śāntideva's *Guide to the Bodhisattva's Way of Life* in Tibetan, see the translator's introduction to Śāntideva, *The Bodhicaryāvatāra*, trans. by Kate Crosby and Andrew Skilton.

34. It is important to appreciate the right context for statements such as this. Many of the thought processes suggested here are rele-

vant principally to those practitioners who have chosen to lead the single-pointed, celibate life of a hermit, for whom the issue of gaining total freedom from attachment to the concerns of this life is of vital importance.

35. Tib. *Gtsang gi btsan.* Tsang is a region in central Tibet, while a *tsen,* translated here as "ghost," refers to aggressive spirits of dead people. Chengawa is probably alluding here to some popular myth about the irritable temperaments of these so-called *tsen* ghosts of the Tsang region, who are easily offended by perceived slights and thus people need to be extremely cautious with them.

36. A succinct biography of Phuchungwa can be found in Lechen's *Lamp Illuminating the History of the Kadam Tradition,* pp. 267a–270a; and see, *Mind Training: The Great Collection,* pp. 423–29.

37. The Tibetan text of this sentence is oblique, and my translation here is merely suggestive.

38. I have read the Tibetan *zho re* as an abbreviation of *zho gang re.* A *shogang* is an old Tibetan coin made of copper.

39. As its name implies, a wish-granting cow fulfills the wishes of its owner, like the genie in Aladdin's lamp. The wish-granting cow, along with the heavenly horse and treasure vase mentioned below, are mythical objects that are often imagined in standard Buddhist rites of offering, especially the mandala offering wherein the entire cosmos is offered to the object of refuge.

40. The brief biographical note presented here on Khamlungpa is drawn from Lechen's *Lamp Illuminating the History of the Kadam Tradition,* pp. 206–7; on "mind training in eight sessions," see *Mind Training: The Great Collection,* pp. 225–37.

41. A brief biographical information on Ben Güngyal as well as a selection of some of his more memorable sayings can be found in Lechen's *Lamp Illuminating the History of the Kadam Tradition,* pp. 223–26.

42. *Treasury of Gems,* pp. 257–64; a succinct biography of Kharakpa as well as a selection of some of his more well-known sayings can be found in Lechen's *Lamp Illuminating the History of the Kadam Tradition,* pp. 226–30.

43. This brief biographical note is drawn from Lechen's *Lamp Illuminating the History of the Kadam Tradition*, p. 205.

44. Lechen (*Lamp Illuminating the History of the Kadam Tradition*, pp. 231–46) provides detailed biographical information on Neusurpa, including citations from some of his teachings.

45. Thupten Jinpa, *Essential Mind Training* (Boston: Wisdom Publications, 2011), pp. 103–26; Lechen's *Lamp Illuminating the History of the Kadam Tradition* (pp. 446–49) provides a brief biography of Langri Thangpa.

46. Lechen's *Lamp Illuminating the History of the Kadam Tradition* (pp. 464–73) provides a very useful biography of Sharawa, while the *Treasury of Gems* (pp. 338–74) gives extensive extracts from numerous writings of this important Kadam master.

47. The primary audience for these instructions is monk practitioners living as hermits in solitary places.

48. Lechen (*Lamp Illuminating the History of the Kadam Tradition*, pp. 330–42) provides an extensive biography of Jayülwa followed by the names of the successive abbots of Jayül Monastery.

49. This short biographical sketch of Master Tölungpa is drawn from Lechen's *Lamp Illuminating the History of the Kadam Tradition*, pp. 324–28.

50. This brief biographical note on Nambarwa was drawn from Lechen's *Lamp Illuminating the History of the Kadam Tradition*, pp. 665–68.

51. This brief biographical note is drawn from Lechen's *Lamp Illuminating the History of the Kadam Tradition*, p. 449.

52. This echoes the well-known Kadam saying that was earlier attributed to Chengawa. See page 65 above.

53. The original Tibetan text reads, "If one pursues the dried meat of this life's desire . . ." The author is probably evoking the analogy of eating dried meat, which, because of its dryness and saltiness, makes one thirsty, and once that thirst is quenched, more craving for the meat arises.

54. None of the historians of Kadam tradition—Sönam Lhai Wangpo, Lechen, Paṇchen Sönam Drakpa, and Jamgön Amé—nor Yeshé Döndrup give Lhopa's personal name. *Lhopa* literally means "southerner," one who is from the south.

55. This brief biographical note on Geshé Lhopa is drawn from Lechen's *Lamp Illuminating the History of the Kadam Tradition*, pp. 230–31, and *Treasury of Gems*, pp. 268–69.

56. Although this is supposed to be part of a set of four, there are only three items. Unfortunately, in all existing versions of the Tibetan text one item is missing from this list.

57. In all editions of the Tibetan text at hand one item is missing from this set. The "wisdom-knowledge empowerment" is the third main empowerment of the highest yoga class of tantra and involves offering a consort to the initiates for entering into sexual union as part of the empowerment rite. The initiate typically only visualizes this empowerment.

58. This last item probably refers to articles belonging to the monastic community. If such items are inappropriately used for one's personal benefit, it is said to be like consuming burning fire.

59. All existing Tibetan versions list this heading as "Five sets of six" despite the fact that they all actually present six sets of six. Here I have modified this caption to fit with the actual list.

60. This is an epithet for the Buddha, in whose presence a Mahayana practitioner takes the bodhisattva vows.

61. All existing versions of the Tibetan text contain only five items on this supposed list of six.

62. The phrase "manifest movement" (*mngon du 'gyu ba*) is probably equivalent to the term *mngon du phyogs pa*, "approaching." The latter is the standard name of the sixth bodhisattva level, which marks a critical stage in the practitioner's direct realization of emptiness of all phenomena.

63. The expression "innate path" probably refers to the Vajrayana path, in which the concept of innateness, especially the fundamental innate mind of clear light, occupies a significant place in the understanding of the nature of the path to full awakening.

64. The "*imputed nature*, the *dependent nature*, and so on" here refers to the Three Natures theory central to Yogācāra analysis of the ultimate nature of reality.

65. This list is taken from Yeshé Döndrup's *Treasury of Gems* (pp. 410–16), where they are listed as the "eighty assorted points" of

Chegom. At the end of these lists, Yeshé Döndrup states that altogether there are in fact 108 such points but that, given the archaic nature of the language in which they were found, he chose not to list them all.

66. At the level of "heat," the first of the four stages of the path of preparation, the practitioner gains meditatively derived insight into emptiness on the basis of yoking together tranquil abiding and penetrative insight. This is not the direct perception of emptiness, but it goes beyond mere intellectual understanding and serves as a condition for the later nondual experience.

67. As noted above, this short introductory essay on the *Book of Kadam* and its spiritual legacy has been adapted from my introduction in *The Book of Kadam: The Core Texts*, which appeared as volume 2 of *The Library of Tibetan Classics*.

68. *The Book of Kadam: The Core Texts*, p. 93.

69. *Book of Kadam*, vol. II, chap. 2, p. 42.

70. *Book of Kadam*, vol. II, chap. 5, p. 160.

71. *Book of Kadam*, vol. II, chap. 19, p. 485.

72. *Book of Kadam*, vol. II, chap. 19, p. 487.

73. For discussion of this second identification, see Franz-Karl Ehrhard, "The Transmission of the Thig-le bcu-drug and the Bka' gdams glegs bam," pp. 29–30 and 51. Lechen Künga Gyaltsen (*Lamp Illuminating the History of the Kadam Tradition*, 2a2) also briefly mentions this tradition of identifying the three Kadam brothers with the three Avalokiteśvara icons in Tibet that are traditionally believed to be self-arisen—that is, they arose naturally as icons rather than being fabricated by artists.

74. In the testament, Atiśa visits Lhasa cathedral with his attendant Naljorpa and does not mention Dromtönpa by name. Leonard van der Kuijp ("The Dalai Lamas and the Origins of Reincarnate Lamas," p. 24) argues that since the testament does not mention Dromtönpa, it may have evolved in an environment where Dromtön and the tradition growing out of his teachings initially had no stake. This suggests, according to van der Kuijp, that the nineteenth chapter of Dromtönpa's birth stories can be seen as a means of establishing Songtsen Gampo as one of Dromtön's previ-

ous births. Whatever the truth of this suggestion may be—which will only be able to be determined when we have accurate dates for the two texts—the two texts are clearly intimately connected.

75. *Kakholma Testament*, p. 319. This testament, as well as the *Book of Kadam*, especially chapters 5 and 19 of the Son Teachings, need to be studied carefully alongside another important treasure text, the *Sacred Collection on Maṇi [Mantra] (Ma ṇi bka' 'bum)*, the discovery or revelation of which is traditionally attributed to Nyangral Nyima Öser (1124–92). Together these texts appeared to have played a key role in propagating many aspects of the myth of Avalokiteśvara and his special destiny with Tibet, beliefs that became deeply ingrained and widespread among the Tibetan people. My own feeling is that the *Kakholma Testament*, at least in its archaic form, predates both the *Book of Kadam* as well as the *Sacred Collection on Maṇi*. In fact, the two latter texts represent subsequent attempts to connect the myth of Avalokiteśvara's special role in Tibet with two important figures in the development of Buddhism in Tibet—the first with Dromtönpa and the second with Padmasambhava. For a brief yet insightful study of the *Sacred Collection on Maṇi*, see Mathew Kapstein, "Remarks on the Maṇi bka' 'bum and the Cult of Avalokiteśvara in Tibet" in Steven D. Goodman and Ronald M. Davidson, eds., *Tibetan Buddhism: Reason and Revelation* (Albany: State University of New York Press, 1992).

76. For more on the origins of the *Book*, consult my introduction to *The Book of Kadam: The Core Texts*.

77. See, for example, Thuken Losang Chökyi Nyima, *Crystal Mirror of Philosophical Systems*, p. 112.

78. Panchen Sönam Drakpa, *History of Old and New Kadam Schools*, 18a3.

79. Ibid.

80. Yeshé Tsemo, *Wondrous Garland of Excellent Jewels*, p. 84b5.

81. Lechen, *Lamp Illuminating the History of the Kadam Tradition*, p. 787.

82. Strictly speaking, the Great Fifth was not the first to relate the two books—the *Kakholma Testament* and the *Book of Kadam*—

outside the texts belonging to the Kadam collection. For example, we see the following comment in Yeshé Tsemo's biography of Gendün Drup (p. 4b6): "Furthermore, there are many similar statements. Later, too, numerous indirect indications will come to light. As for the details, however, one needs to understand them from the *Precious Book* and the *King's Testament*."

83. Desi Sangyé Gyatso, *Yellow Beryl: A History of the Ganden Tradition*, for example, p. 365. This project of equating the Great Fifth with Avalokiteśvara, and with previous successive emanations of the Buddha of Compassion, especially with figures like Dromtön and the previous Dalai Lamas, is extensively developed in Desi's voluminous supplement to the Great Fifth's autobiography, *Fine Silken Robe*.

84. For an analysis of the dynamic interrelations between the myth of Avalokiteśvara, Tibet, and the Dalai Lamas, see Leonard van der Kuijp's "The Dalai Lamas and the Origins of Reincarnate Lamas" in Martin Brauen, ed., *The Dalai Lamas: A Visual History* (Chicago: Serindia, 2005), pp. 14–31.

85. By referring to these beliefs as "myths," I do not mean to contrast them with some kind of "reality" and suggest that they are somehow false. I am using the term in a sense that defines myth broadly as a story whose main figures are personalities—divine, human, or even animal—who accomplish something significant for their adherents. See Robert A. Segal, *Myth: A Very Short Introduction* (New York: Oxford University Press), p. 4.

86. The text lists seven specific purposes of Dromtönpa assuming his present existence as someone with a Tibetan nomadic background. See *The Book of Kadam: The Core Texts*, p. 67.

87. See, for example, Thupten Jinpa, *Essential Mind Training* (Boston: Wisdom, 2011), p. 31.

88. Drom is here classifying the well-known twelve links of dependent origination, often depicted as the "wheel of life," into causes, conditions, and effects with respect to a sentient being's karmically conditioned birth in the cycle of existence.

89. Here the text uses the Tibetan term *khrims*, which means "law," "rule," "regulation," or a "norm." Admittedly, the usage of this term

here is somewhat peculiar. Perhaps it should be read as meaning "rules of usage in language" or "established linguistic convention." Thus, speaking of tasting the mind as if it were a food would violate normal linguistic convention.

90. These lines are from the *Bodhisattva's Jewel Garland*.

91. "Lady" and the "white youth" here refer to Tārā and Avalokiteśvara.

92. What follows in the subsequent lines is almost the entire instruction found in the mind-training work entitled *Leveling Out All Conceptions* (*Mind Training: The Great Collection*, chapter 12 [root text], and chapter 32 [commentary]). Interestingly, here Atiśa attributes the instruction to his teacher Avadhūtipa, whereas in *Mind Training* it is attributed to Serlingpa.

93. In the root text of *Leveling Out All Conceptions* in *Mind Training*, this line reads slightly differently, "Carry forth the force of all antidotes."

94. These lines are from the *Bodhisattva's Jewel Garland*.

95. These lines are from the *Bodhisattva's Jewel Garland*.

96. The following lines appear to have been added by an editor who compiled the teachings together as a single text. Although the Tibetan text of these particular stanzas is somewhat obscure, after paying homage to Dromtönpa as Avalokiteśvara (hence the reference to Buddha Amitābha on his crown), the editor makes the following interesting points. First, he states that the root-text summary that encapsulates all the themes of the dialogue is without doubt Master Atiśa's own work. He then goes on to say that the collected dialogues between Atiśa and Dromtönpa stand apart (*logs su bkol ba*) as a collection in their own right, though no title was given to them by Atiśa. The editor then asserts that the teachings contained here are clearly dialogues on Atiśa's *Bodhisattva's Jewel Garland*, although in this root text no queries and responses have been specified. This is followed by the remark that, upon embracing the words of Master Atiśa, the teachings were instantly written down. This is probably an allusion to the story of Ngok Lekpai Sherap being the scribe when Atiśa repeated to him the entire dialogue once again. Finally, the editor says that it was written in "the Bodhgaya style"; it is difficult to discern whether

the editor means that it was originally written in some central Indian script or whether he is referring to a literary style.

97. The entire text of the preamble of the Son Teachings is found in the opening section of chapter one, namely the first birth story. An English translation of this story and stories 2, 20, and 22 can be found in *The Book of Kadam: The Core Texts.*

98. This is a reference to Mount Lhari Nyingpo, which according to the opening of the *Jewel Garland of Dialogues* is located upon Tārā's right leg.

99. This is Naljorpa Amé Jangchup, who served Atiśa as a personal attendant and later succeeded Dromtönpa as the head of Radreng Monastery.

100. This is an allusion to Khutön's reputation as a somewhat prideful teacher. It is said that when Dromtönpa wrote a letter inviting the great figures of the Tibetan Buddhist world from central Tibet to come to formally receive Atiśa, he failed to include Khutön's name. This offended Khutön, who is reputed to have exclaimed, "I am not someone who is to be counted in the 'and so forth's,'" and went ahead of the group to meet Atiśa.

101. Lotsāwa, or "translator," refers here to Ngok Lekpai Sherap.

102. In all the redactions of the *Book of Kadam*, a sentence or two appears to be missing here. Because of this, the connection between this reference to a paṇḍita and the story that follows is not immediately apparent.

103. There are several different redactions of these animated-corpse stories in Tibetan. Though attributed to Nāgārjuna, the individual stories within the collection are strikingly indigenous Tibetan in their character.

104. These lines are from the *Bodhisattva's Jewel Garland.*

Glossary

accumulations. *See* two accumulations.

antidote (*gnyen po*). Just as specific medicines are identified as antidotes for specific illnesses, specific mental states such as compassion, loving-kindness, and so on are identified as antidotes against specific mental ills. The Tibetan term *gnyen po* is sometimes translated as "remedy" or "counterforce" as well.

awakening mind (*byang chub kyi sems, bodhicitta*). An altruistic aspiration to attain buddhahood for the benefit of all beings. The awakening mind is characterized by its *objective*, the full awakening of buddhahood, and its *purpose*, the fulfillment of others' welfare. Often another term, *mind generation* (*sems bskyed*), is used to refer to awakening mind as well. *See also* two awakening minds.

awareness (*rig pa, vidya; shes pa, jñā*). As a verb both Tibetan terms *rig pa* and *shes pa* mean "to know," "to be cognizant of," and "to be aware." When used as a noun, *shes pa* is often translated as "consciousness" or "mental state," while *rig pa* is translated as "awareness," suggesting the most basic quality of subjective experience. In the *Book of Kadam*, the source of our volume, the Tibetan term *rigpa* (translated as "awareness") is primarily used in the sense of "the basic quality of awareness."

bodhisattva (*byang chub sems dpa'*). A person who has cultivated the awakening mind and is on the path to buddhahood.

conceptualization (*rnam rtog, vicāra*). The Tibetan term *rnam rtog* has been translated as "conceptualization" and carries numerous connotations: (1) it can refer simply to thoughts, which unlike sensory experiences are mediated by language and concepts; (2) it can also, however, refer specifically to dichotomizing thoughts that lead to objectification and reification of things and events; and (3) the term may sometimes be used in a negative sense to mean "false conceptualization." In the context of this volume, *rnam rtog* (conceptualization) carries more the second and third meanings.

conqueror (*rgyal ba, jina*). A common epithet used to refer to a fully awakened buddha. When capitalized in this volume, in most cases it refers to the historical Buddha. The term also serves as a frequent epithet for Atiśa in the *Book of Kadam*.

cyclic existence (*'khor ba, saṃsāra*). The perpetual cycle of birth, death, and rebirth conditioned by karma and affliction. Freedom from cyclic existence is characterized as *nirvana*, the "transcendence of sorrow."

dharmakāya (*chos sku*). Literally meaning "truth body" or "buddha body of reality," the term refers to the ultimate reality of a buddha's enlightened mind—unborn, free from the limits of conceptual elaboration, empty of intrinsic existence, naturally radiant, beyond duality, and spacious like the sky.

emptiness (*stong pa nyid, śūnyatā*). According to the philosophy of emptiness, all things and events, including our own existence, are devoid of any independent, substantial, and intrinsic reality. This emptiness of intrinsic existence is phenomena's ultimate mode of being—the way phenomena actually are. Seeing emptiness, the ultimate nature of all things, is understood to be an indispensable gateway to liberation and enlightenment.

four divinities (*lha bzhi*). The four chosen divinities of the Kadam teachings: (1) the Buddha, the teacher of the doctrine, (2) Avalokiteśvara, the divinity embodying compassion, (3) Tārā, the divinity embodying enlightened action, and (4) Acala, the protective divinity.

four immeasurable thoughts (*tshad med bzhi, caturapramāṇa*). Immeasurable (1) compassion, (2) loving-kindness, (3) sympathetic joy, and (4) equanimity.

Great Compassion (*thugs rje chen po, mahākaruṇā*). When capitalized in this work, it is an epithet for Avalokiteśvara, the buddha of compassion, specifically in his thousand-armed manifestation.

Mahayana (*theg chen, mahāyāna*). Literally "Great Vehicle," this term refers to the form of Buddhism most prominent today in Himalayan countries and East Asia. The Mahayana tradition is distinct from non-Mahayana Buddhism in idealizing the path of the altruistic bodhisattva, who practices in order to free all suffering beings rather than merely to secure his own personal nirvana.

method (*thabs, upāya*). *Method*, when paired with wisdom, refers to the altruistic deeds of the bodhisattva, including the cultivation of compassion and the awakening mind, the practice of the first five of the six perfections, and the accumulation of merit through making offerings, prostrations, and prayers to the enlightened beings and through serving one's teacher. In Mahayana Buddhism, the union of method and wisdom is central to understanding the path.

noble one (*'phags pa, ārya*). A being on the path who has gained a direct, nonconceptual realization of the truth of emptiness. Noble ones are contrasted with ordinary beings (*so so'i skye bo, pṛthagjana*), whose understanding of the truth remains bound by language and concepts.

perfection of wisdom (*sher phyin, prajñāpāramitā*). One of the six perfections that lie at the heart of the practice of the bodhisattva. The term refers also to a specific subdivision of Mahayana scriptures that outline essential aspects of meditation on emptiness and its associated paths and resultant states. *The Perfection of Wisdom in Eight Thousand Lines*, the *Heart Sutra*, and the *Diamond Cutter* are some of the most well-known Perfection of Wisdom scriptures. In the *Book of Kadam* the term is often used as an epithet for Mother Perfection of Wisdom, a feminine divinity that embodies the perfection of wisdom of a fully awakened buddha. *See also* six perfections.

pratyekabuddha *(rang sangs rgyas)*. "Self-enlightened ones," who seek liberation on the basis of autonomous practice as opposed to listening to other's instructions. *See also* śrāvaka.

pith instructions *(man ngag, upadeśa)*. Sometimes translated simply as "instructions," *man ngag* (pith instructions) connotes a specialized kind of advice, such as instruction suited only to a select class of practitioners. Often the Tibetan term *man ngag* also refers to an oral tradition.

samsara. *See* cyclic existence.

self-grasping *(bdag 'dzin, ātmagrāha)*. Instinctively believing in the intrinsic existence of your own self as well as of the self-existence of external phenomena. "Self" here means a substantial, truly existing identity. The wisdom that realizes emptiness eliminates this self-grasping. *Self-grasping* is a synonym for *ignorance*.

seven limbs *(yan lag bdun)*. A popular Mahāyāna Buddhist rite of worship made up of the following seven elements: (1) paying homage, (2) making offerings, (3) confessing and purifying negative karma, (4) rejoicing in virtuous deeds, (5) supplicating the buddhas to turn the wheel of Dharma, (6) appealing to the buddhas not to enter into final nirvana, and (7) dedicating one's merit.

six perfections *(phar phyin drug, ṣaṭpāramitā)*. The perfections of (1) giving, (2) morality, (3) forbearance, (4) joyful perseverance, (5) concentration, and (6) wisdom. These six perfections constitute the heart of the bodhisattva's practice, especially with respect to the perfection of his or her own mind.

śrāvaka (*nyan thos*). Followers of the Buddha who have as their primary spiritual objective the attainment of liberation from the cycle of existence. The Sanskrit term and its Tibetan equivalent are sometimes translated as "hearers" (which stays close to the literal meaning) or as "pious attendants." *Śrāvakas* are often paired with *pratyekabuddhas*, or "the self-enlightened ones."

sugata (*bde bar gshegs pa*). Literally, "one gone to bliss"; an epithet for a buddha.

tantra (*rgyud*). Literally, "continuum," *tantra* refers to a highly advanced system of thought and meditative practice wherein the very aspects of the resultant state of buddhahood are brought into the path right from the start. Unlike the general practices of Mahayana, engagement in the meditative practices of tantra requires prior initiation into the teachings. The term *tantra* can also refer to the literature or tantric texts that expound these systems of thought and practice.

three baskets (of scripture) (*sde snod gsum, tripiṭaka*). Refers to a threefold classification of all the teachings attributed to the Buddha: (1) the discipline basket (*vinaya piṭaka*), (2) the discourses basket (*sūtra piṭaka*), and (3) the higher knowledge basket (*abhidharma piṭaka*). The *Book of Kadam* emphasizes the need to subsume all the teachings of the Buddha within this threefold collection of scriptures and undertake their practice.

three doors (*sgo gsum*). Body, speech, and mind—the three avenues for activity, both enlightened and worldly.

three (higher) trainings (*bslab pa gsum, triśikṣā*). The higher trainings in morality, meditation, and wisdom. Each constitutes the principal subject matter of the scriptural collections on discipline (*vinaya*), discourses (*sūtra*), and higher knowledge (*abhidharma*), respectively. The entire Buddhist path is subsumed into these three higher trainings.

Three Jewels (*dkon mchog gsum, triratna*). The Buddha Jewel, the Dharma Jewel, and the Sangha Jewel. Together, these three constitute the true objects of refuge in Buddhism. You take refuge in the Buddha as the true teacher, in the Dharma as the true teaching, and in the Sangha (the spiritual community) as true companions on the path.

twelve links of dependent origination (*rten 'brel bcu gnyis, dvādaśāṅgapratītyasamutpāda*). (1) Ignorance, (2) karmic formations, (3) consciousness, (4) name and form, (5) sense bases, (6) contact, (7) feeling, (8) craving, (9) grasping, (10) becoming, (11) birth, and (12) aging and death. According to Buddha's teaching of the law of cause and effect, it is through an unending interwoven chain of these twelve links that an individual revolves within the cycle of existence conditioned by karma and affliction.

two accumulations (*tshogs gnyis*). Wisdom and merit, the accumulations of which are essential for the attainment of buddhahood. The accumulations of these two constitute the heart of the path to full awakening, with the first, wisdom, pertaining to ultimate truth while the second, merit—referred to also as "method"—relating to conventional truth.

two awakening minds (*sems bskyed gnyis*). Following the Indian Mahayana Buddhist classics, the Kadam texts such as the *Book of Kadam* speak of "two awakening minds," or "two bodhicittas"—conventional and ultimate. The former refers to the altruistic intention defined above under *awakening mind*, while the latter refers to a direct realization of the emptiness of the fully awakened mind. In general usage, *awakening mind* is a synonym for the conventional awakening mind.

ultimate expanse (*chos dbyings, dharmadhātu*). A synonym for ultimate nature. Calling it "expanse" invokes the space-like quality of the ultimate mode of being of all things.

ultimate nature (*gnas lugs*). Refers to the ultimate mode of being of things, which for a Mahayana Buddhist is *emptiness*.

upāsaka (*dge bsnyen*). A Buddhist practitioner who has taken the lay-person vows, committing to observe some or all of the five principal precepts against (1) killing, (2) stealing, (3) engaging in sexual miscon-duct, (4) telling lies, and (5) using intoxicants. As Dromtönpa chose to remain a lay practitioner, he is often referred to in the *Book of Kadam* as Upāsaka. An *upāsikā* (*dge bsnyen ma*) is female practitioner with such a vow.

Vajrayana. *See* tantra.

wisdom (*shes rab, prajñā*). The Sanskrit term *prajñā* and its Tibetan equivalent *shes rab* have different applications depending upon the context. In the Abhidharma taxonomy of mental factors, *prajñā* refers to a specific mental factor that helps evaluate the various properties or qualities of an object. The term can refer simply to intelligence or men-tal aptitude. In the context of the Mahayana path, *prajñā* refers to the wisdom aspect of the path constituted primarily by deep insight into the emptiness of all phenomena. Hence the term *prajñā* and its Tibetan equivalent *shes rab* are translated variously as "wisdom," "insight," or "intelligence."

Yama (*gshin rje*). The lord of death.

Bibliography

Āryadeva. *Four Hundred Stanzas [on the Middle Way]. Catuḥśatakaśās-tra. Bstan bcos bzhi brgya pa.* Toh 3846, dbu ma *tsha.* P5246, *tsha.* An English translation of this work with extant fragments of the San-skrit original can be found in Karen Lang's *Āryadeva's Catuḥśataka* (Copenhagen: Akademisk Forlag, 1986). A translation of the root text from the Tibetan edition with Gyaltsap Je's commentary can be found under the title *The Yogic Deeds of Bodhisattvas: Gyel-tsap on Āryadeva's Four Hundred*, trans. and ed. Ruth Sonam (Ithaca: Snow Lion Publications, 1994).

Atiśa Dīpaṃkara. *Bodhisattva's Jewel Garland. Bodhisattvamaṇevalī. Byang chub sems dpa' nor bu'i phreng ba.* Toh 3951, dbu ma *khi.* P5347, *ki.* An English translation is found in Thupten Jinpa, trans., *The Book of Kadam: The Core Texts.*

Book of Kadam. Bka' gdams glegs bam. 2 vols. Typeset edition, Xining: Nationalities Press, 1993.

Brauen, Martin, ed. *The Dalai Lamas: A Visual History.* Chicago: Ser-india Publications, 2005.

Buddhagoṣa. *The Path of Purification (Visuddhimagga).* Translated from the Pāli by Bhikkhu Ñāṇamoli. Kandy: Buddhist Publication Society, 1991.

Chattopadhyaya, Alaka. *Atīśa and Tibet.* Delhi: Motilal Banarsidass, 1967; reprint ed. 1999.

Chenga Lodrö Gyaltsen (1402–72). *Initial Mind Training: Opening the Door of Dharma. Thog ma'i blo sbyong chos kyi sgo 'byed.* Xylo-graph edition reprinted in *Three Texts on Lamrim Teachings* (Dha-ramsala: Library of Tibetan Works and Archives, 1987).

Das, Sarat Chandra. "The Lamaic Hierarchy of Tibet." *Journal of the*

Buddhist Texts Society of India 1 (1983): part I, 31–38; part II, 44–57.

Decleer, Hubert. "Master Atiśa in Nepal: The Tham Bahīl and Five Stūpas according to the *'Brom ston Itinerary*." *Journal of the Nepal Research Centre* 10 (1996): 27–54.

Desi Sangyé Gyatso (1653–1705). *Yellow Beryl: A History of the Ganden Tradition. Dga' ldan chos 'byung bai dru rya ser po.* Typeset edition, Xining: Nationalities Press, 1989.

Ehrhard, Franz-Karl. "The Transmission of the *Thig-le bcu-drug* and the *Bka' gdams glegs bam*." In *The Many Canons of Tibetan Buddhism*, edited by Helmut Eimer and David Germano, 29–56. Leiden: Brill, 2002.

Gö Lotsāwa Shönu Pal (1392–1481). *Blue Annals. Deb ther sngon po.* 2 vols. Typeset edition, Sichuan: Nationalities Press, 1984. English translation by George N. Roerich in *The Blue Annals* (Calcutta: Royal Asiatic Society of Bengal, 1949–53). Latest reprint Delhi: Motilal Banarsidass, 1988.

Jinpa, Thupten, trans. *Essential Mind Training.* Boston: Wisdom Publications, 2011.

———, trans. *Mind Training: The Great Collection.* The Library of Tibetan Classics 1. Boston: Wisdom Publications, 2005.

———, trans. *The Book of Kadam: The Core Texts.* The Library of Tibetan Classics 2. Boston: Wisdom Publications, 2008.

Kakholma Testament. Ka chems ka khol ma. Typeset edition, Kansu: Nationalities Press, 1989.

Kapstein, Mathew. "Remarks on the Maṇi bka' 'bum and the Cult of Avalokiteśvara in Tibet." In *Tibetan Buddhism: Reason and Revelation*, edited by Steven D. Goodman and Ronald M. Davidson. Albany: State University of New York, 1992.

Lechen Künga Gyaltsen (fifteenth century). *Lamp Illuminating the History of the Kadam Tradition. Bka' gdams chos 'byung gsal ba'i sgron me.* Typeset edition, Tibetan Nationalities Press, Lhasa, 2003.

Pabongka Rinpoche. *Liberation in the Palm of Your Hand.* Edited by Trijang Rinpoche. Translated by Michael Richards. 2nd ed. Boston: Wisdom Publications, 2006.

Paṇchen Sönam Drakpa (1478–1554). *History of the Old and New*

Bibliography

Kadam Schools: Beautiful Ornament for the Mind. Bka' gdams gsar rnying gi chos 'byung yid kyi mdzes rgyan. Xylograph edition of Potala Library reprinted in *Two Histories of Kadam School* published by Gonpo Tseten in Delhi, 1977.

Pawo Tsuklak Trengwa (1504–66). *Joyful Feast for the Learned: A History of Buddhism. Chos 'byung mkhas pa'i dga' ston.* 2 vols. Typeset edition, Beijing: Nationalities Press, 1985.

Śāntideva. *Guide to the Bodhisattva's Way of Life. Bodhicaryāvatāra. Byang chub sems pa'i spyod pa la 'jug pa.* Toh 3871, dbu ma *la.* P5272, *la.* English translations include Stephen Batchelor's *Guide to the Bodhisattva's Way of Life* (Dharamsala: Library of Tibetan Works and Archives, 1979), the Padmakara Translation Group's *Way of the Bodhisattva* (Boston: Shambhala Publications, 1997), Alan and Vesna Wallace's *Guide to the Bodhisattva's Way of Life* (Ithaca: Snow Lion Publications, 1997), and Kate Crosby and Andrew Skilton's *Bodhicaryāvatāra* (New York: Oxford University Press, 1995).

Segal, Robert. *Myth: A Very Short Introduction.* New York: Oxford University Press, 2004.

Thuken Losang Chökyi Nyima (1737–1802). *Crystal Mirror of Philosophical Systems: A Tibetan Study of Asian Religious Thought.* Translated by Geshé Lhundrub Sopa. Edited by Roger R. Jackson. Boston: Wisdom Publications, in association with the Institute of Tibetan Classics, 2009.

van der Kuijp, Leonard. "The Dalai Lamas and the Origins of Reincarnate Lamas." In *The Dalai Lamas: A Visual History*, edited by Martin Brauen, pp. 14–31. Chicago: Serindia Publications, 2005.

Yeshé Döndrup (1792–1855). *Treasury of Gems: Selected Anthology of the Well-Uttered Insights of the Teachings of the Precious Kadam Tradition. Legs par bshad pa bka' gdams rin po che'i gsung gi gces btus legs bshad nor bu'i bang mdzod.* Typeset edition, Kansu: Nationalities Press, 1995.

Yeshé Tsemo (b. 1433). *Wondrous Garland of Excellent Jewels: A Biography of the Glorious All-Knowing Gendün Drup. Thams cad mkhyen pa dge 'dun grub pa'i dpal gyi rnam thar ngo mtshar rmad 'byung nor bu'i phreng ba.* Collected Works of the First Dalai Lama, xylograph, Tashi Lhünpo edition, vol. *ka*; TBRC scanned version, vol. *ca.*

Index

About Thupten Jinpa

THUPTEN JINPA was trained as a monk at the Shartse College of Ganden monastic university where he achieved the highest rank of Geshe Lharampa, and he holds a BA in philosophy and PhD in religious studies both from Cambridge University. He has been the principal English-language translator for His Holiness the Dalai Lama for more than two decades and has translated and edited numerous bestselling books by the Dalai Lama. Jinpa's own works include *Self, Reality and Reason in Tibetan Philosophy* and several volumes in *The Library of Tibetan Classics* as well as *Essential Mind Training*. An adjunct professor at McGill University, a scholar at the Center for Compassion and Altruism Research and Education (CCARE) at Stanford University, Jinpa is also the Chairman of the Mind and Life Institute. He is the president of the Institute of Tibetan Classics in Montreal, where he lives with his wife and two daughters, and is the general editor of *The Library of Tibetan Classics*.

About Wisdom Publications

WISDOM PUBLICATIONS is dedicated to offering works relating to and inspired by Buddhist traditions.

To learn more about us or to explore our other books, please visit our website at www.wisdompubs.org.

You can subscribe to our e-newsletter or request our print catalog online, or by writing to:

Wisdom Publications
199 Elm Street
Somerville, Massachusetts 02144 USA

You can also contact us at 617-776-7416 or email us at info@ wisdompubs.org.

Wisdom is a nonprofit, charitable 501(c)(3) organization, and donations in support of our mission are tax deductible.

Wisdom Publications is affiliated with the Foundation for the Preservation of the Mahayana Tradition (FPMT).